PAINTING &
EMBROIDERY
ON SILK

PAINTING & EMBROIDERY ON SILK

Jacqueline Taylor

CASSELL

to Barry and David

A CASSELL BOOK

First published in the UK
1992 by Cassell
Villiers House
41/47 Strand
LONDON
WC2N 5JE

Distributed in the United States
by Sterling Publishing Co., Inc.
387 Park Avenue South, New York, NY 10016-8810

Distributed in Australia
by Capricorn Link (Australia) Pty Ltd
P.O. Box 665, Lane Cove, NSW 2066

British Library Cataloguing in Publication Data

Taylor, Jacqueline
Painting & embroidery on silk.
I. Title
746.6

ISBN 0 304 34133 9

Typeset by Litho Link Limited, Welshpool, Powys, Wales.
Printed and bound in Hong Kong by Dah Hua Printing Press Co. Ltd.

Contents

Acknowledgements

My special thanks are due to Barry Thomas, who took the colour photographs and who helped with all aspects of the book.

I should also like to thank Mike Evans, who took the black and white photographs; Jackie Edwards for her typing and her patience; and the following artists for permitting me to use their work: Doreen Harrison (colour photograph 15), Alison Holt (colour photograph 14), Lynda Jowers (colour photograph 30), Enid Leckie (Fig. 78, box), Liz Rowlands (colour photograph 6), John Waring (colour photograph 9), Caryl Webb (colour photograph 20) and Julie Wilson (Fig. 78, scarf).

I am grateful to Christopher Neukom for allowing me to use reference material, photographs and the work of his late wife, Mary Neukom (colour photograph 18).

The following kindly let me use examples of my work in their possession: Stuart Blackmore, Gill Cowhig, Barry and Sarah Dixon, David and Evelyn Jones, Joan May, John and Eluned Morris, Lorna Sawyer, Ruby Smith, Hazel Stubbs and May Thomas.

I should also like to acknowledge with grateful thanks the help of Peter Ellerington, who made all my frames; Marjorie Hall; Bill and Enid Leckie, who checked the original manuscript; my friends, Roy and Lorna Sawyer, who offered constant encouragement and support; my father, David Smith, who assisted with the research; Dave Thomas and Sheila Ockenden, who modelled some of the garments; Roger Boniface, Brian Jones and the staff of Bebington High School for their kind support; the staff of Cassell who have been most patient and helpful; and last, but not least, my mother, who encouraged me to draw and paint.

Introduction

My aim in writing *Painting & Embroidery on Silk* has been to introduce newcomers to the enjoyable and fascinating pastime of decorating silk.

First produced in China more than two thousand years ago, real silk has a luxuriousness and strength that artificial fibres cannot match. There is, too, an astonishing variety in the kinds of silk fabric that are available. This book is designed to encourage you to take advantage of the properties of this delightful material and to decorate it and use it in a host of attractive ways.

The basic equipment you will need is readily available in craft shops or the haberdashery departments of many large stores, and, because patterns and designs can be traced on to silk, no great artistic skills are necessary. If you do enjoy sketching and drawing, I am sure you will find that painting on silk in the media of silk paints and gutta will be both rewarding and challenging.

The exercises included in the pages that follow have been specially devised and tested – over many years and with students of a wide range of ages and abilities – to help beginners to develop confidence and expertise. As you work through them, you will learn how to apply different types of paint – including those specially manufactured for painting on silk and fabric paints – and gutta, and the ways in which different types of silk can be used to achieve a variety of effects.

There are also exercises to help you gain confidence in the use of colour, and I have included suggestions on mixing and blending colours so that you will be able to produce subtle and arresting patterns and designs.

Spraying techniques range from the use of a simple mouth diffuser to a sophisticated compressor-driven airbrush, but both can be used to produce wonderfully shaded and patterned backgrounds. Using masks and stencils, you will quickly find that you can produce some stunning results. I also suggest ways in which you can combine the techniques of spraying, painting and drawing with a gutta nib using fabric paint to create striking and effective designs.

Some unusual effects can be obtained by using salt or dishwasher crystals together with silk paints, and I explain the processes involved in detail. They are well worth experimenting with, and I am sure you will produce some marvellous results.

Painted silk designs can be further enhanced by stitches, and I have included detailed information on the ways in which both hand and machine embroidery can be used in conjunction with painted silk backgrounds. Hand embroidery, for example, can embellish and add detail to a painting in which gutta has been used for the outlines so that the background can be seen through the stitches and the painted and stitched areas complement each other.

Machine embroidery has become increasingly popular in recent years, and most sewing machines have an embroidery foot. I have included a comprehensive explanation of the techniques involved in machine embroidery and describe the ways in which the embroidery facility on sewing machines can be used to produce a variety of effects.

I have also included a description of how you might develop a landscape of your own, and how you could work from your original source materials – sketches, perhaps, or photographs – to the finished picture, building up the image from the original painted background to the addition of embroidered details.

There is also a section on using painted silk in unusual ways on garments and accessories. A simple design on painted silk can be appliquéd to a T-shirt, or, as you gain experience, you might want to make a padded bag or even a waistcoat.

I hope that, as you work through the exercises in this book, you will come to enjoy this fascinating process as much as I do. Do not be put off if any of the techniques appear complicated. Choose a simple project to begin with – a greetings card, for example – and follow the instructions. You will be surprised at how easily you are able to achieve some professional-looking items, and in no time you will be producing beautiful cushion covers, pictures and garments.

The best way of keeping up to date with suitable suppliers of equipment and materials is to read through the advertisements in current issues of general crafts and embroidery magazines.

1 Equipment and Materials

Silk paints are wonderful media with which to work. Simple techniques can be combined in different ways to produce an astonishing variety of rich or subtle images and designs. The range of silk paints available offers an almost limitless number of colours and the widest range of tones. There are also some excellent fabric paints in a variety of colours that can be used, either on their own or in conjunction with silk paints, to create different effects.

Perhaps the most exciting aspect of painting on silk is the versatility of the process. You can make a brilliantly coloured card or paint a unique design on a scarf or blouse. If you enjoy embroidery you can combine a variety of embroidered foregrounds and middlegrounds with different background effects painted or sprayed on the silk. Stencils and masks can be used to great effect, and painted or sprayed silk can be quilted in many interesting ways using machine or hand stitching.

The techniques involved in painting on silk are very straightforward and easy to master. The paints can be used in a free-hand way, similar to the water-colour technique in which paint is allowed to flow freely across the fabric. In colour photograph 1, for example, a cloud effect was achieved by applying the paint directly on the silk, while the details were embroidered by machine.

The paints can also be used with a resist medium known as gutta. When an area – a leaf or flower, for instance – is enclosed or outlined by gutta, the paint applied inside the shape is confined by the gutta, which acts as a barrier and prevents paint bleeding. Applying gutta is not difficult, although it requires practice. The various uses and types of gutta are discussed in detail later in this chapter.

The exercises outlined in Chapter 2 will help you to develop your basic skills in painting on silk so that you can combine them with other techniques. The exercises have been tried and tested with students of a very wide range of age and ability. The projects described in this book vary in difficulty, but if

you work through the exercises first, progressing gradually from one technique to the next, your expertise will develop over a period and you will be able to produce some beautiful items of your own.

TYPES OF SILK

Obviously, different items call for different types of silk. If you are simply painting a picture that will be framed, you can use any weight of silk you like. Lightweight silks are cheaper and will enable you to achieve a painterly effect more easily.

If you are making a garment, a heavier weight is necessary. Heavyweight habutai is suitable for ties or waistcoats, for example, but if you are making clothes, such as scarves or blouses, you must use a silk that falls or drapes well, and crêpe de Chine is perfect in this respect.

If you like to work on a cream coloured silk, antung is ideal for cushions. It is a robust fabric, suitable for machine embroidery. The creaminess of the silk does not lend itself to the water-colour technique if you want to paint a sky, leaving white areas showing for cloud effects, but it is fine for sprayed skies and backgrounds, especially when you work with a powerful diffuser. If you like the texture, you can buy bleached antung.

Different paints give different results on each type of silk, and your selection of silk will depend on the effects you want to achieve. For example, colours painted on antung will look more muted and less vibrant than those painted on white habutai. The vibrant effect of colour on white habutai can be seen in colour photograph 2, where ornamental cabbages have been used as the basis for the designs.

Takobar is another very versatile silk. It is an ideal material for painted backgrounds for machine embroidery as it is strong and can withstand repeated layers of machining. In addition, if you are painting free-hand you will find that it is easier to control the paint on takobar and that it does not spread as much as paint applied to habutai.

There are many types of silk you can work with, and I have mentioned only those with which I have had most success. Experiment with different kinds until you find a silk and type of paints that give you the results you want and that you enjoy working with. The choice is yours.

Wherever you buy your silk, it is important to make sure that it is ready for use. If the manufacturer describes it as ready prepared, you can go ahead and not worry about shrinkage. If you are in any doubt, however, rinse the silk thoroughly or you may, for example, find that your cushion does not fit the pad after washing.

Washing silk can be tricky. It is a delicate fabric, and you must treat it properly. Wash it gently in warm water in a mild detergent that does not contain any bleach. Roll it in a towel to remove the excess water and iron it on the reverse of the design while the silk is damp. Do not use the steam setting on your iron, or you may get watermarks on the silk and have to wash it again.

1 *A Landscape with Thrift* The detail was added by machine embroidering on top of the painted silk.

SILK PAINTS

Unless they are restrained by gutta or an inhibitor that has been painted on the silk first, silk paints will spread rapidly over the fabric, merging with one another and creating translucent effects.

Several types of silk paint are available. Some must be fixed by steam, and these are normally used with a solvent-based gutta; others are fixed either by chemicals or by ironing, and they are usually used with a water-based gutta. Examples of each type are described below, but beginners should experiment with the paints that are fixed by chemicals or by ironing because steam fixing either requires more expensive equipment or the items have to be sent away to be fixed professionally. When gutta is not required and fixing is not necessary – that is, if the painted article will never require washing – it is possible to use any type of paint or paints together.

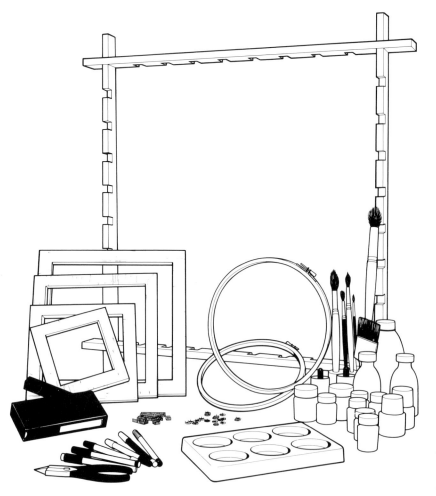

Fig. 1   Some of the equipment you will need – a selection of paints and brushes and a palette to hold the paint while you work, together with a range of different-sized frames. In the centre are some silk pins, which you will need to hold your fabric firmly to the frame.

Deka paint

Deka paints are water-based and can be mixed easily to create different colours and tones. Pastel shades can be achieved simply by adding water or white silk paint. These paints are ideal for beginners of all ages as they are easy to handle and are non-toxic. They are fixed by ironing the back of the fabric with the iron on a medium heat. You should place a clean cloth under your work to separate the silk from the surface of your ironing-board.

Orient Express paint

The colours available in the Orient Express range of paints are rich, and some vibrant effects can be created by using the colours undiluted. The paints can be mixed and blended easily, and when paint is overlaid – that is, when colours are painted on top of each other – they give lovely, glowing results. The paints are fixed by immersing the silk in a bath of a proprietary fixative: 1fl oz (25ml) of fixative is added for every 2 pints (1 litre) of water used, and the water has to be at a temperature of 68°F (20°C). Total immersion is necessary, and you will find a large plastic box or tray ideal for the purpose.

Both Deka and Orient Express paints come in small bottles with screw tops. At first I found it difficult to put the paint into the palette in the small quantities that are needed, but I overcame this by using a pipette for each colour. Orient Express paints now have a pipette fixture attached to the top of the jar, which is very convenient. If you do not want to use a pipette, you can dip a stick – the non-bristle end of a paintbrush, for example – into the jar to take up a very small quantity of paint and deposit it on your palette.

If you want to keep the colours you have mixed, you will need lots of small glass jars with screw-top lids. You can buy these from chemists, order them from chemical suppliers or ask your friends to collect miniature preserve jars for you, as these are ideal.

Kniazeff and Du Pont paints

These are types of steam-fixed paints, which have to be diluted with alcohol, methylated spirits or water. There is a wide selection of colours available in each range, and when the paints are fixed they are extremely lustrous. Du Pont paints give good results when painted with alcohol. The silk should be painted and left to dry, and then patterns can be created by painting on to the dry silk with alcohol. It is also possible to combine these paints with other makes – for example, mix Du Pont or Kniazeff with Deka or Orient Express paints – to use as a background. It is worth experimenting with different combinations, but remember to keep a record so that you can repeat an effect you particularly like.

FABRIC PAINTS

Fabric paints give quite different effects from silk paints. They do not spread and merge like silk paints, but give a matt finish whether they are painted straight on to the silk or over silk paint. Like gouache or water-colour paints, fabric paints have to be diluted with water to alter their consistency. Their effect is somewhat similar to gouache, but unlike gouache, fabric paints do not become brittle and crack when they are sewn into. Another advantage is that you can paint over errors quite easily.

Deka permanent fabric paint

Deka permanent fabric paints are easy to mix, they spray well, and they can be fixed easily by ironing. There is a wide range of colours, including gold and silver, and the metallic white can be used to create lustrous effects in designs, especially when spraying. Like most silk paints, they are available in handy jars of approximately 1fl oz (25ml), but they are also available in larger size jars.

Pebeo opaque fabric paint

You may sometimes require fabric paint to cover dark silk backgrounds, and Pebeo opaque paint is useful for this purpose as it does not allow the background colour to show through.

BRUSHES AND PALETTES

You can buy special brushes for painting on silk, but I have found that any good paintbrush does the trick. You will need a wide selection of sizes so that you have the correct one to cover a particular area quickly to avoid streaking or flooding. Wide foam brushes are also available, and these are useful when you want to cover large areas evenly. Fine brushes that do not carry too much paint are essential for filling tiny areas and for detailed work.

Never put too much paint on your brush. A heavily loaded brush will encourage bleeding, and because silk paint spreads so easily and quickly in small areas you do not need a great deal. You may decide to use a different brush for each colour, but it is easy to get them muddled up unless you are working with a limited palette of only two or three colours.

As with any type of painting, the more tones you use the more interesting your work will be, so you may find it useful to pre-mix some paint with water in several suitable containers with airtight lids. Different proportions of paint to water create different strengths of colour: the more water you add, the paler the tone of the colour will be. If you prepare a range of shades, you will have strong colour to mix straight out of the bottle and some diluted tones separately available.

Spotless equipment is essential for silk painting. Use kitchen roll or tissue to dry your brush when you wash it before changing colour, as any water or colour on the brush will dilute or alter the colour you want to use. It is essential to prevent cross-colour contamination. The paints are so strong that frequent changes of water are necessary. You should, therefore, keep several pots of water on your work table and change them often.

Different types of palette are available. If you are using a small amount of paint, a flat surface will do, but if you are working with larger quantities, a palette with compartments will be more useful. You will also need a selection

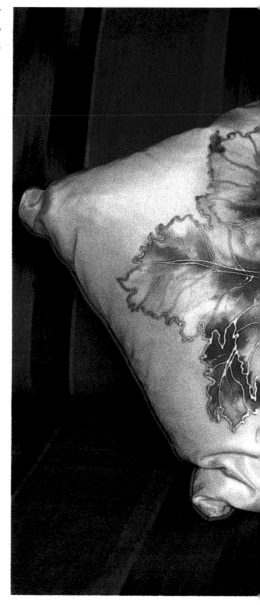

2   Ornamental cabbages painted with
Orient Express paints on habutai silk.

of glass or plastic containers of suitable proportions to hold the paint for dipping, for piping and so on.

FRAMES

Frames are essential items of equipment. In an early attempt to paint a scarf, I worked without stretching the silk on a proper frame – with disastrous results. Because the silk was not taut enough, the gutta lines were wobbly, and when I came to paint the silk the paint ran over the uneven surface and caused streaks.

If you are planning to paint a large piece of silk you will need to use a fairly high frame. An adjustable one, similar to the one shown in Fig. 1, is ideal for this, and you can purchase this kind of frame quite readily. For small items, old picture frames are a good substitute. A cheap way of making a set of frames is to buy a sheet of ⅖in (1cm) plywood and have it cut into solid frames, about 1in (2.5cm) wide, decreasing in size as illustrated in Fig. 1.

Sand the frames down, and they are ideal for painting or for machine embroidery as the fabric can be fixed in place using either silk pins for painting or staples to give the tension necessary for machine embroidery. The frames you use for silk painting can be as large as you want, but for embroidery you will be limited to the size your machine will accommodate.

Embroidery frames of all sizes are useful for painting on silk, and the wooden ones especially are quite cheap to buy. Bind the rings with fabric strips or cotton tape to prevent the silk from slipping while you work.

SILK PINS

These circular pieces of metal with three prongs are pushed almost flush into the frames. They are easy to remove and replace and enable you to adjust the silk on the frame with little difficulty. Although they are perfect for painting on silk, they do not hold the material securely enough for machine embroidery.

STRETCHING SILK

If you are going to silk paint only, take a frame and cut or tear the silk so that it is large enough to cover the frame up to the edges. It is best to pin each corner first, stretching the silk gently but firmly. Try to keep the grain of the fabric straight. Then pin the middle of opposite sides, still stretching the silk. Continue to place the pins in the centre of each group of pins until the silk is quite taut and the pins are at intervals of approximately 1in (2.5cm) (Fig. 2).

For machine embroidery you will have to staple the silk to a frame, and this must be done after the fabric has been painted and allowed to dry thoroughly. The silk must be larger than the frame because an overlap is needed to make sure that it is stapled securely in place. This procedure is described in detail in Chapter 5.

GUTTA

Gutta is a resist medium that is available in different types and colours.

Water-based gutta

Water-based gutta is the easiest and best kind for beginners to use. There are five main types – transparent (which can be either washed away to leave the background colour of the silk or left in a picture or on a greetings card as a white outline), and silver, black, gold and assorted colours. These opaque guttas leave a raised line on the silk, and they are fixed by ironing the reverse side of the fabric for three minutes. For example, I used silver gutta to outline the ornamental cabbage on the cushion shown in colour photograph 3.

You can use several types of gutta in one picture if you want to create

Fig. 2   Use silk pins to stretch the silk across the frame.

Fig. 3   Bottles of gutta and, in the foreground, the special applicator nibs.

particular effects. I often use transparent gutta on its own because it is possible to achieve subtle, more painterly effects as the gutta merges with the painting. Coloured gutta is often best used to highlight certain parts of a painting or to add a detail. For example, a little black gutta could be used to emphasize the centre of some anemones, or touches of gold gutta could be added to leaves or foliage.

3   A detail of one of the cushions in colour photograph 2, showing the silver gutta used to outline the individual shapes.

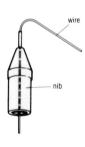

Fig. 4   An empty plastic bottle with a nozzle.

Fig. 5   A gutta nib with a length of wire through it to prevent the nib getting clogged with dry gutta.

Fig. 6   Cut off the nozzle with a sharp knife.

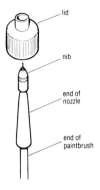

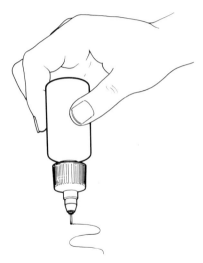

Fig. 7   Inserting the nib into the bottle top.

Fig. 8   The nib should fit securely into the hole in the bottle top.

Fig. 9   Draw a few lines on a piece of scrap paper to make sure that the gutta is flowing smoothly before you begin to apply it to your piece of silk.

Fig. 10   As soon as you have finished, clean the nib by rinsing it in running water, using an old paintbrush to remove every last trace of gutta, and wash it in soapy water.

Fig. 11   When you are satisfied that the nib is as clean as possible, replace the wire.

Solvent-based gutta

This type of gutta is petroleum-based, and it must be thinned with alcohol or methylated spirits. It is generally used in conjunction with steam-fixed paints, and it has to be coloured with typographic ink unless you buy one of the already coloured kinds that are now available.

Applying gutta

Gutta can be applied in different ways. Some types are supplied in bottles with nozzles, which can be pierced with a pin. I have seen some artists using this to draw with, but it tends to give a rather wide, cumbersome line. It is better to use a special nib, which will give more control. These nibs vary in width, and you can draw very thin lines with the smallest of them (size 5). There are two main ways of applying gutta nibs to applicator bottles (Fig. 3).

Method 1

Take an empty plastic bottle with a nozzle (Fig. 4) and a gutta nib. Keep a length of wire in the nib when it is not in use to prevent clogging (Fig. 5). Remove the wire and put it away in a safe place. They are easily lost, and I have wasted a lot of time looking for wires because I failed to put them away in one place.

Take the top off the bottle and cut off the nozzle at the point indicated in Fig. 6; a sharp craft knife is ideal for this job. Insert the gutta nib into the bottle top and push it up, using the end of a paintbrush or something similar. You might find it helpful to place the part of the nozzle you cut off on top of the paintbrush and use it to push the nib through the hole (Fig. 7). As you push, firmly but gently, the pressure of the paintbrush will force the nib into the aperture (Fig. 8). The top is now ready to be transferred to a bottle containing gutta.

Make sure that there are no air bubbles in the bottle by gently squeezing the gutta into the neck of the bottle. Firmly screw on the top with the nib and turn the bottle upside down. Hold it at a comfortable angle and draw some lines and shapes on a spare piece of paper before you begin to apply it to silk (Fig. 9).

When you have finished clean the nib. Do this immediately you have finished whenever possible to prevent the gutta drying in the nib. Rinse it under the tap (Fig. 10) and wash it in soapy liquid. I use an old paintbrush to make sure that all traces of gutta are flushed away, and I blow through the nozzle to make sure it is not clogged. Finally, replace the wire in the nib (Fig. 11) and keep all your nibs soaking in a jar of water to prevent any remaining gutta from drying out. You will, of course, need a spare top to replace the one you have the nib in, or you can pour the gutta into a bottle that has a top.

Method 2

Take a bottle of gutta that has a nozzle and use a sharp knife to cut off the tip of the nozzle (Fig. 12). Place the gutta nib neatly over the top of the nozzle (Fig. 13). To prevent any leaks and secure the nib, wrap masking tape over the join of the nib and nozzle (Fig. 14).

When you have finished using the gutta, remove the masking tape and wash the nib thoroughly, remembering to replace the wire. Place the plastic cap over the end of the nozzle so that the gutta remaining in the bottle does not dry out.

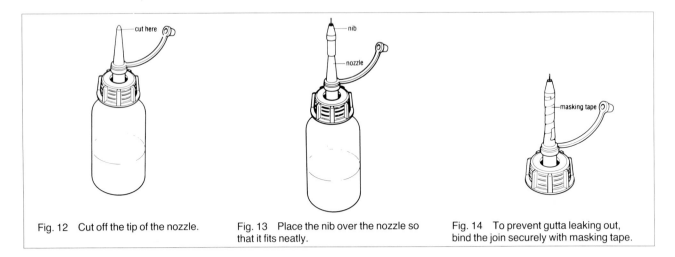

Fig. 12   Cut off the tip of the nozzle.

Fig. 13   Place the nib over the nozzle so that it fits neatly.

Fig. 14   To prevent gutta leaking out, bind the join securely with masking tape.

Using a cone

Another way of applying gutta is by using a cone made from paper. These are popular with professional artists, and it is possible to achieve fine, flowing lines. The advantages of cones are that they are cheap, disposable, create no air bubbles and don't stretch the silk. However, the successful use of a cone comes only with practice and confidence.

Cones can be constructed in the following way using glassine, greaseproof or tracing paper. Cut a piece of paper to approximately 8 × 6in (20 × 15cm), and, taking opposite corners on the top left and bottom right of the paper, roll the right-hand corner over the left-hand corner to create a cone (Fig. 15). Moisten your fingers and pull the inside of the cone to create a fine point (Fig. 16). Pushing will create a wide point. Apply glue to the flap beneath the cone (Fig. 17) and glue the flap at the point of the cone, to secure it. Insert a pencil in the cone and use it to get rid of any bumps and to make sure the inside is completely smooth (Fig. 18). When you are sure that the cone is smooth, pour in the gutta (Fig. 19), then flatten the top of the cone and fold over the corners (Fig. 20). Fold the top down several times and fasten it with tape when you cannot fold it any more (Fig. 21). The pressure exerted as you fold down the top of the cone may be sufficient to force out the gutta, but if it does not, insert a needle or pin in the pointed end to release the gutta, which can be applied to your design (Fig. 22). Replace the pin when you have finished or put the gutta back in a container and make a new cone when you are ready to continue.

Apart from using it for outlines or highlights, gutta can be used in other

4   This poinsettia was painted on silk within an outline of transparent gutta that had been drawn over the outline made by a blue marking pen.

ways. You may, for example, want to block out an area of fabric so it remains white while you apply paints to the rest. In this case you should use a brush to apply the gutta. If you are in a hurry to paint your design, you can use a hair-drier, but it is best to let gutta dry naturally if you intend to wash it out. Heat can embed it in the fibres of the silk.

PENS FOR USE ON SILK

There are three types of pen that can be used to draw outlines on silk. One kind, which is both water- and air-soluble, is available in pink or in purple. This is very useful for drawing outlines for pictures and landscapes as the

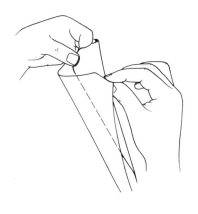

Fig. 15   Roll the bottom right-hand corner over the top left-hand corner of the rectangle of paper to form a cone.

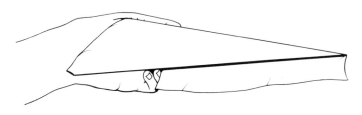

Fig. 16   Carefully pull the inside of the corner to make a sharp point.

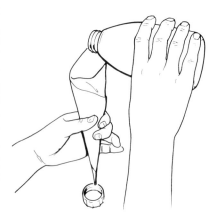

Fig. 19   Slowly pour some gutta into the cone.

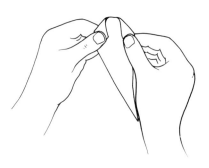

Fig. 20   Fold over the top corners of the cone.

Fig. 21   Continue to fold down the cone as far as you can, then hold the top in place with a piece of adhesive tape.

image disappears gradually over a period of hours or immediately if water is applied to it. This miraculous little pen, which is made by Madeira, is invaluable. Madeira also produces a fabric pen with an eraser at one end.

The other type of pen that can be used effectively to mark silk is a blue pen, but it is water-soluble only. This kind of pen is useful for giving a clear and lasting line on items that will be washed. Sometimes the blue outline can be partly washed out by painting while the remaining traces of blue are left in because they can look quite attractive, as can be seen in colour photograph 4. You must be careful not to apply heat to the fabric before the blue line is removed or it may leave a stain when the item is washed. These pens should not, therefore, be used on articles that require heat fixing.

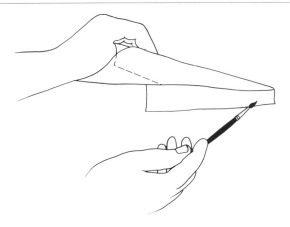

Fig. 17   Apply a little glue to the flap under the cone.

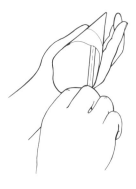

Fig. 18   Use a pencil to make sure the inside of the cone is completely smooth.

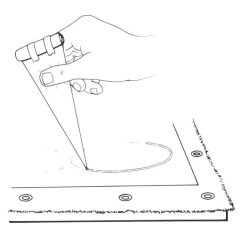

Fig. 22   The pressure exerted as you fold down the top of the cone may be sufficient to force out the gutta, but if the gutta does not flow readily through the tip of the cone, insert a pin or needle into the hole until the gutta is released.

5 The highlights on the petals of the
crocuses are clearly visible.

2 Using Gutta, Silk Paint and Fabric Paint

Before you begin any work you should practise with the equipment and materials if they are new to you. The exercises outlined in this chapter for working with silk paints and fabric paints have helped students to overcome basic problems with techniques, but it is important to bear in mind that the exercises will be most useful when they are applied instinctively as a result of practice and as part of a creative process rather than mechanically, as an initial exercise must, inevitably, tend to be used.

APPLYING GUTTA AND SILK PAINT

Stretch a piece of lightweight habutai over a frame approximately 8 × 12in (20 × 30cm). With the frame silk side up, trace or copy the shapes in Fig. 23 in water-soluble ink or with a 'disappearing' pen. The shapes to be traced should show clearly through the thin silk, even though the silk is a frame's depth from the outlines on the page.

Take a small bottle and attach a narrow nib to the top as described in Chapter 1. Outline the shapes you have traced, holding the gutta pen as shown in Fig. 24. You can test to see if you have applied the gutta properly by painting near the edges of the shapes with water. If the water spreads through the gutta, dry it off quickly with a hair-drier and re-apply the gutta. If your paint still bleeds, it will probably be because you have overloaded your paintbrush. You can minimize the effect of bleeding by immediately diluting the paint with water, dabbing it with cotton wool buds or with kitchen paper and drying with a hair-drier.

Fig. 25 shows the completed exercises. Beginning with the first shape (Fig. 23a), try to paint each petal with a different tone of one colour. Use only a small amount of silk paint as it spreads quickly and mix undiluted paint with varying amounts of water. Use a small brush, size 02 for small areas. Note how the paint goes paler when it dries. If you want to strengthen the colour in

Fig. 23   Trace or copy these outlines on to a
piece of silk.

part of the design, wet the whole area and re-apply the paint.

In the second shape (Fig. 23b) use the same colour paint but try to make
one petal stand out from another by using light and dark tones against each
other. Do not be put off if you find that the whole shape floods and creates a
flat effect as in the previous shape. This will happen when you have too much
paint on your brush. If you act quickly when you have flooded an area you can
remove some paint with a cotton wool bud or a paper towel wrapped around
the end of a brush. Dry your brush on a paper towel and dip it into the paint.
Paint one edge of the petal. Quickly clean the paint off your brush and dip it
in water. Make sure there is only a little water on the brush and blend the
paint as shown in Fig. 26. Practise controlling the paint and water, and you
will soon find that you can easily create a smooth range of tone from light to
dark. Notice that the tonal effect in this second shape is much more effective
than the flat colour in Fig. 23a.

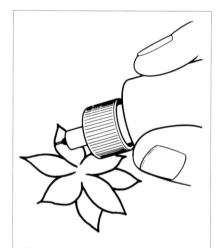

Fig. 24   Holding the gutta applicator as
shown, draw the outlines of the shapes
you have traced.

Different tones or strengths of colour are essential for a successful painting. First, of course, a flat colour without any tone can be boring and limit the effectiveness of a design. Second, when you want to create a three-dimensional or solid effect, tones are necessary. In addition, if you are painting a landscape, the colours in the foreground are usually much bolder than those in the background. To create a successful composition you will have to create pale and strong tones and control your paints carefully.

To paint the third shape (Fig. 23c) use two colours – red and yellow or red and blue, for example. Paint the petals as you did in Fig. 23b, but then overpaint carefully in another colour. You will see a lovely effect as the two colours blend. You can overlay colour in this way as many times as you like to create a variety of effects. To prevent tide- or watermarks forming, remember to wet, but not saturate, the whole area first.

Fig. 27 shows three shapes with extra paint worked in. The left-hand and

Fig. 25   The completed exercises.

Fig. 26   Blending paint – you will need very little water on your brush.

centre shapes have tidemarks because the paint was not blended properly; the third shape shows an even blending.

When you come to paint the fourth shape (Fig. 23d) experiment by adding dots and splashes of colour inside the shapes. Let some of them blend into each other naturally and try to blend others with your brush.

In the fifth shape (Fig. 23e) try to create a three-dimensional effect by painting each side of the leaf in a different tone. Remember that you can paint over an area with more paint to strengthen the colour but that you must do this while the first layer of paint is damp or you must cover the whole area with a little water first.

Try to create a highlight in the sixth shape (Fig. 23f) by leaving a tiny area white. Highlights are those areas where light falls on an object, and in paintings or drawings these areas are usually left as light as possible. In the picture of crocuses, colour photograph 5, the highlighted areas on the petals can be clearly seen.

The hydrangea picture, colour photograph 6, was completed as a first attempt at painting on silk after the exercises outlined above had been mastered. It is a lovely example of what is possible, and the slight bleeding adds to the charm.

Fig. 27   The shapes on the left and in the centre have tidemarks because the paint was not blended properly; the right-hand shape shows what can be achieved.

APPLYING FABRIC PAINT

You can practise blending fabric paints on any type of fabric – cotton or calico, for example – so that you can save your silk for an important piece if you wish. You will need to stretch the fabric on a frame. Embroidery frames are ideal and are less trouble to use because you do not have to staple or pin the material.

6   Gold gutta was used on this delightful painting of hydrangeas.

Fig. 28 shows a range of exercises that employ fabric paint in various ways.

Mixing graded pale tones

The pattern at top left of Fig. 28 (see page 32) was created by mixing three colours with white to give a gradual change of tone. Take some white fabric paint, shaking the bottle first. You will need about as much as will comfortably cover your thumbnail. Mix the paint in a clean palette to get an even consistency. Then take a primary colour – blue, for example – and place a small amount in another compartment of your palette. Using a small brush, take some white and paint a line on the cloth. Clean your brush and dry it, then add a very small amount of blue to the white. A subtle change of tone should be visible: the white should have become palest blue. Paint a line of this next to your white line.

Repeat the process, drying and cleaning your brush each time. The white will eventually become saturated by the blue, but between the blue and white

should be a graduated range of tones. Do not worry if you cannot get it perfect the first time. Very few people do.

Repeat the process with all the primary colours. If you prefer, draw a shape and paint the lines within it, or you could use undulating or jagged lines.

Mixing dark tones

Similar stages can be followed to mix the dark tones shown in the top right-hand pattern in Fig. 28. Take some blue paint and place a small amount in your palette. Mix to a good consistency and paint a line on your cloth. You can make a line pattern if you wish.

Place some black in your palette and, using a clean brush, add a very small amount of black to the blue. Black saturates colours very quickly so you will not need to use much to alter the primary colour. Paint a second line next to the first one.

Continue to work in this way until the primary colour has changed from pure blue through blue/black, black/blue to black. Again, you should achieve a graduated range of dark tones.

Repeat the process for all the primary colours. Some people prefer not to use black for dark tones, and if you wish you can use very dark blue or dark purple. Experimentation will show you what you can achieve.

Mixing secondary colours

Working with secondary colours is really enjoyable, and you will soon be able to create some eye-catching patterns such as the one at centre left in Fig. 28.

Place some yellow paint in a clean palette. Paint a yellow line on your cloth, or, if you are filling in a shape, paint a line at the edge of the shape. Add a very small amount of blue, and the yellow should change from pure yellow to a very pale yellowy-green.

Continue to add very small amounts of blue until the yellow becomes saturated. You should have achieved a range of colours gradually changing from yellow to green to blue.

If your pattern of lines or shape is complete, start a new one but still use the blue paint. Take some red, preferably crimson as scarlet will create a brownish-purple, and add it to the blue so that you achieve a graduated range of colours from blue through purple to red.

Repeat the process, this time adding yellow to red so that you create a range of oranges from yellow-orange through red-orange to red.

Creating a three-dimensional effect

Now try blending colours to create a ribbon-like effect going from light to dark. In the example shown at centre right in Fig. 28 only the primary colours with white for the highlight were used. Remember that when you are using silk paints, the background white fabric has to show through to create a highlight, but when you are working with fabric paints you can use the paint to make a highlight. In some ways fabric paints are easier to use as you have more control.

Fig. 28   Using fabric paints.

Using fabric paint with a gutta nib

Select any colour you like and half fill a gutta bottle with fabric paint. It is important to use a very fine nib. Make sure the top is on securely and practise on a piece of paper before drawing on the silk, which should, of course, be stretched before you begin. You can create many sorts of patterns on the silk – see, for example, the pattern at bottom left in Fig. 28. If you want to build up colours, wait for the fabric paint to dry and then work over the top. Working wet on wet can cause smudging.

Using fabric paint with a gutta nib on a painted silk background

It is possible to use silk paints and then to work into the background using fabric paint with the gutta technique. In the example at bottom right of Fig. 28 the gutta nib was used to enhance the painted silk background design with linear effects.

As you can see, these exercises in the use of fabric paints by themselves or in combination with silk paints have a lot of possibilities for design – and they are also fun to do.

Tertiary colours

Tertiary colours, which are obtained by mixing the three primaries, are extremely useful, and, depending on the proportions of blue, red and yellow you mix, a very wide range of colours can be created.

A useful experiment is to mix together the secondaries – purple, orange and green – in various combinations. You can also mix primaries with secondaries – blue with orange, for example. The resulting colours will contain all the primaries but one or two colours may predominate. For example, if you mix the secondary colour purple, which is composed of blue and red, with green, which is composed of blue and yellow, you will have a tertiary colour in which blue predominates. If you mix purple and green and add red, you will have a colour composed of two parts red, two parts blue and one part yellow. However, if you add blue to orange, red to green or yellow to purple you may have a more even balance of blue, red and yellow.

To experiment with the tertiaries I divided my frame into nine compartments (Fig. 29). Then I used a fabric pen to draw a pattern of curved and spiral shapes over the whole area. In the first box (top left) I mixed orange with green, adding green little by little to create gradual changes of colour. I filled in the pattern by building up lines of colour, but I left some areas white. Before the orange became saturated with green, I began to add white gradually to create pale tones and used these to paint more line patterns, following the drawn outlines.

In the second box (centre top) I again mixed orange and green, but then gradually added blue. When I had added enough blue, I began to add white to create some pastel tints. For the third box (top right) I also mixed orange and green, but this time I gradually added yellow. When I had added sufficient yellow, I added white and used the resultant tints to build up the pattern.

7 *A Garden Path* The path was painted with fabric paint, while the rest of the background was painted with silk paint. The detail was added with machine embroidery.

35

In the centre row of boxes I followed the same procedure but worked with purple and green. For the box at centre left I gradually added green to purple, then introduced white. For the centre box I mixed purple and green, then added red. Before the mix was saturated with red, I added white. For the box at centre right I added blue to the mixture of purple and green, before adding white as before.

In the bottom row I mixed orange and purple. In the bottom left box I built up colours by adding orange to purple, then introducing white. In the centre box I added yellow to the purple and orange, then added white as before, and in the bottom right box I added red to the purple and orange before adding white.

By varying the proportions of the primary colours used and mixing the colours gradually in this way I was able to create a wide range of tertiary colours. The traced pattern served as a sort of grid, and the complete exercise is a handy colour reference. You will be surprised at the number of browns and greens you can mix. I find that the best results can be achieved by mixing the secondaries from the primaries rather than by using ready-mixed colours.

In the detail of the machine embroidery shown in colour photograph 7, the garden path was painted with fabric paint while the rest of the background was worked in silk paint, which formed a background for the stitched foliage and complemented the colours of the stitching.

Fig. 29   Using fabric paints to create tertiary colours.

3 Starting a Project – Cards and Pictures

Bearing in mind the experience and skills you have so far acquired and the exercises you have completed, you can now begin to look for a design on which you feel you could enjoy working. It may be a collection of objects from your home – a plant from your garden, set against a fabric you like, for instance – Japanese origami paper or even snail shells. Textiles themselves make excellent starting points, and I have photocopied sections of Javanese batiks and used these as the basis of a design. Colour photograph 8 shows a variety of objects, ranging from natural forms to postcard reproductions, that might inspire a design.

You can use material that you find in magazines or books, or if you have a camera and prefer to use your own photographs, you can obtain really good close-ups by using a dioptre. They are inexpensive and can be fixed on to a single lens reflex camera very easily. I use the plus-4 size, but there are various sizes available.

If you are artistic, drawings and quick sketches provide the most personal and individual source material and often give the best results. On the other hand, if you are not very expert at figurative drawing you can emphasize pattern and colour and not worry too much about anything else. Geometric patterns can look very attractive on both decorative and functional articles, and they demand little drawing skill. In addition, the nature of the silk painting process, in which outlines can be used, allows the drawing process to be bypassed altogether if necessary, as the subject to be painted can be traced on to the fabric.

There is a wealth of information on design sources and methods of developing designs in modern embroidery books, and you should consult any of the books in your local library for further information on this subject.

The one single technique that I use most often is enlarging patterns or designs that I come across. Whenever I find a small sketch or drawing that appeals to me I enlarge it either free-hand or on a photocopier. Modern

8 Some of the many subjects that might form the starting point for a design.

technology is a boon to design in some ways – you can juggle around with photocopies, cutting and pasting them until your design pleases you. However, if you do not have access to a photocopier, you can easily enlarge – or reduce – a shape or illustration by using a diagonal grid as shown in Fig. 30. First, section off the pattern you want to enlarge with a rectangle or square, depending on the shape of the original. Next, draw the diagonals in the box, and then add lines to join the middle of the opposite sides of the box. Then you should draw in the remaining diagonal of each of the quarter sections you have created. Finally, draw a square or rectangle similar in proportion to the original box but as large as you require, and draw in a grid like the first one. Recreate the shape by copying what you see in each section of the grid. There is even no need to use a ruler for this method unless you wish to. Remember that you can use exactly the same process to reduce a shape.

Having chosen a design, you will now have to think about a colour scheme. The key to all successful pieces of work is the combination of colour choice and technique. Some beginners worry unnecessarily about their choice of colour, probably because the selection is almost overwhelming. When you begin it is sensible to keep to a limited palette. The theory of colour has filled volumes, but if you observe the ways in which colour is used in nature and art your sense of colour will develop, and, with practice, you will gain confidence in your choice. If you have doubts about the use of different colours together, look at colour postcards, textiles, ceramics, jewellery or natural forms, all of which will suggest endless colour ranges with which you can experiment. You might find it helpful to look at the way colour is used in famous paintings, and perhaps use these as a basis for your own work. Van Gogh's use of colour opposites is fascinating, for example. According to his letters: 'There is no blue without yellow and without orange, and if you put in blue, then you must put in yellow and orange too, mustn't you?'

If you are always on the look out for colour you will see it in all sorts of places. You can record unusual and striking uses of colour in a photograph or sketch, and it is a good idea to keep your observations on colour from whatever source in a sketch book or notebook, which will, in time, become your own colour reference library.

Many of the personal writings and biographies of artists reveal that, although they nearly always wanted to learn from each other and experiment with each other's methods and styles, most seemed to concur in the opinion that there are no absolute rules or theories that, followed slavishly, will result in fine work. Theories and rules are helpful, but ultimately the artist assimilates them and develops an individual style through practical application and experiment.

Van Gogh described the experience of release from rules and examples in a letter to his brother Theo from Arles, in September 1888. 'Everywhere and all over the vault of heaven is a marvellous blue, and the sun sheds a radiance of pale sulphur, and it is soft and as lovely as the combination of heavenly blues and yellows in a Van der Meer of Delft. I cannot paint it as beautifully as that,

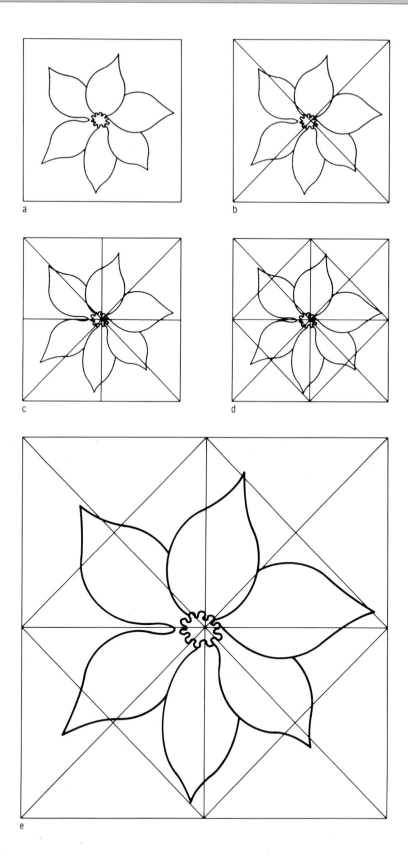

Fig. 30   Individual shapes and patterns can be easily enlarged (or reduced) by using a diagonal grid. First, draw a square or rectangle around the shape (a), then draw in the diagonals (b). Next, draw lines to join the centres of the opposite sides (c) and join the central points by adding diagonal lines in each quarter (d). Finally, draw a larger (or smaller) square or rectangle with the same proportions as the original, and copy what you can see in each section of the grid (e).

41

but it absorbs me so much that I let myself go, never thinking of a single rule.'

Once you feel confident that you can use your materials with some skill, and you have a design and colour scheme you like, you can embark on your first design and enjoy it.

GREETINGS CARDS

Your very first project should be something small – a card would be ideal. You might find it frustrating to attempt something too ambitious when you have not had much experience, and it might put you off silk painting altogether. The first consideration is that your design must fit the frame, so you should draw an outline of the frame in your sketch book. Your design will need to be drawn in coloured pencil or waterproof black felt-tip pen so that you can see it through the silk. When you are using very fine silk you will be able to see your tracing even if the silk is raised by the frame's thickness from the drawing; thicker silk requires a different technique, which is described later in this chapter.

Colour photograph 9, shows a first attempt at making silk cards by a young student, John Waring, who really enjoys painting. First, he drew a still-life of a tradescantia on a patterned fabric background. Then he used a black felt-tip pen to trace a section of the design on a piece of tracing-paper that was slightly larger than the card mount with which he intended to frame his work (Fig. 31). This was repeated for the second design, and each design was enclosed in a rectangle. Next, the two tracings were reversed and taped to the work surface (Fig. 32).

Some silk was stretched over the chosen frame, and the frame was placed on top of the drawings with the silk side down. The shapes were then traced with a 'disappearing' air-soluble pen (Fig. 33). The frame was turned over so

9 The drawing of tradescantia was traced in 'disappearing' pen outlined in transparent gutta, and the gold outline was added afterwards.

Fig. 31 Use a black felt-tip pen to make a tracing of the image.

Fig. 32 Tape the tracings to your work surface to keep them in position reversing them first.

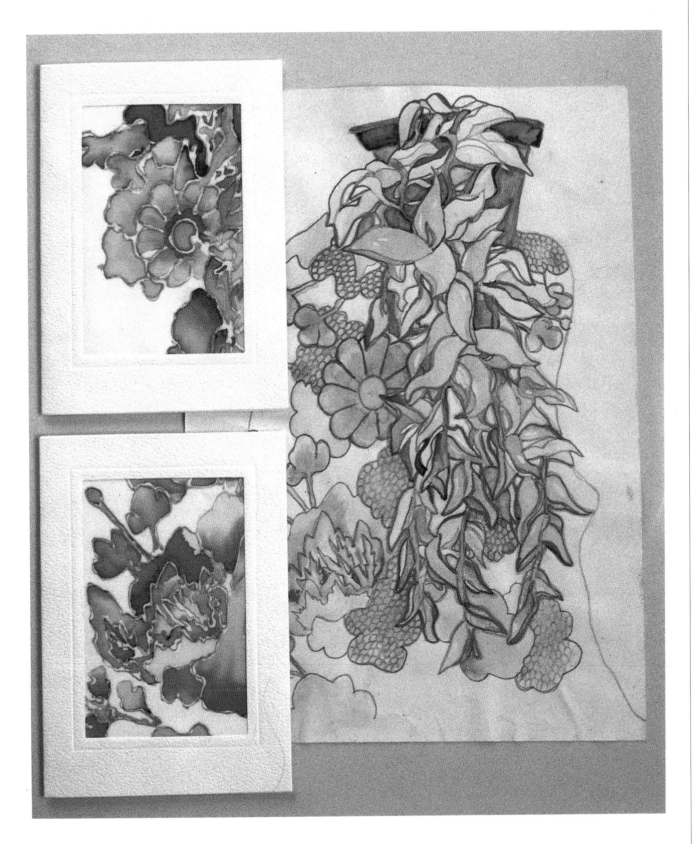

that the silk was raised from the work surface, and the drawings were then outlined in transparent gutta (Fig. 34). If you are making cards like these, make sure that you outline the shape so that paint cannot bleed outside the rectangle that encloses your design.

Working in this way means that the design is reversed when the frame is turned over. If you want to retain the original design, reverse the tracings or place your frame over the drawing with the silk side up and outline it in gutta with the frame separating the silk from the original drawing. Thin silk is quite transparent, so this is not a problem. Alternatively, if you cannot reverse your tracing or drawing, you can re-pin the silk to the top of the frame, although be careful because thin silk does tend to distort if it is adjusted in this way.

Fig. 33   Stretch a piece of fine silk on a frame and use a 'disappearing' pen to trace the picture on the silk.

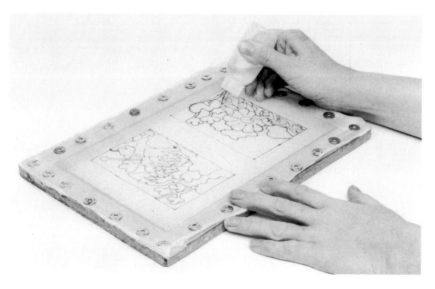

Fig. 34   Use transparent gutta to outline the pattern.

The two cards shown in colour photograph 9 were painted with Orient Express colours, which were overlaid and blended together. Finally, the cards were embellished with gold. It would have been possible to have used gold gutta to start with, and this would have given a neater edge, but the overall impression is, nevertheless, very attractive. If you use the same nib for gold and for transparent gutta, make sure that you clean it thoroughly or you will get traces of gold in your transparent gutta, and these may not wash out.

To finish off the cards some Bondaweb was ironed on to a piece of backing cotton (Fig. 35), the backing paper was peeled off (Fig. 36), and the cotton was ironed to the silk (Fig. 37). Finally, the painting was mounted on to a three-fold card (Fig. 38). This procedure was followed for the second card.

Fig. 35   Iron Bondaweb to a piece of backing cotton.

Fig. 36   Peel away the backing paper from the Bondaweb.

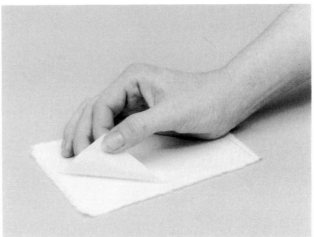

Fig. 37   Iron the cotton to the silk.

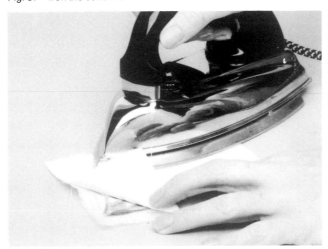

Fig. 38   Mount the finished painting in a free-fold card.

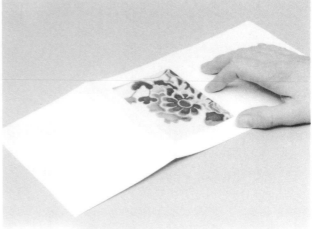

A SMALL PICTURE

Making a small picture is very similar to making a card. When you have selected a design you need to choose a suitably sized frame. As long as the frame will fit over the design you have chosen, you can follow exactly the same steps as for the card, but do make sure you apply gutta all around the edge of the picture to prevent paint bleeding on to the frame.

The silk painting illustrated in colour photograph 10 arose out of my interest in architecture, and I used photographs for reference. I generally find that the more I observe and sketch an object, the better the result is, but although I look at Chester Cathedral very often, I have little time to stand and sketch, so photographs had to suffice. When time is short, photographs can be a great aid.

I was struck by the play of hot and cold colours within the cathedral, and I tried to bring out this element in my colour scheme. I also liked the rhythm of the patterns in the windows, and the leading around the individual lights made me think of gutta lines.

In my first worksheet, which can be seen in colour photograph 10, I experimented with the variety of patterns that is to be found in the stone work and stained glass windows. Although basically Norman, Chester Cathedral contains different architectural styles from various periods, all of which are rich in pattern.

I experimented with a coloured pencil overlay, working layers of colour over each other to try to evoke the effect of the contrast between the vibrant colours of the stained glass and the shadows and silhouettes of the stone work. I developed this study into a simple repeat pattern with a border. The colour scheme contrasted cold blues with warm orange/reds, and the curving nature of the windows and tracery in the repeat pattern contrasted with the zigzag pattern of the border.

Having completed two experimental worksheets, I felt that I was beginning to get the feel of the subject, and at this point I decided that I didn't want a completely symmetrical composition but would rather retain the hot and cold contrast in the colour scheme and the contrast of curved and straight line patterns. Eventually, I redrew my design in a larger, simpler, less symmetrical format so that it would fit a frame 13 × 7½in (33 × 19cm). I also decided to limit my palette to blue, turquoise, red, yellow and orange and used as many blues, reds and yellows as I had available in the Orient Express range. Silver gutta seemed the right choice for the outline as it reminded me of the leaded lights. The design I ended up with is very simple and colourful, and it is not beyond the skill of an inexperienced silk painter.

If you would like to try to work on a similar design of your own, follow the steps outlined here.

First, tape the design (Fig. 39) to your work surface. Then stretch a piece of lightweight silk over a suitably sized frame. When I was working on my design, I traced the outline drawing using an air-soluble pen. The silk will be raised above the design being traced by the thickness of the frame, but if you are using fine silk it is possible to see the outlines clearly through the fabric.

10 *Chester Cathedral* Work sheets and the
finished painting on silk.

47

Fig. 39 The outline drawing for the Chester Cathedral painting illustrated in colour photograph 10.

If you are using a thicker silk and you do not want your drawing to be reversed, you can place the silk next to the drawing to be traced, transfer the outlines to the silk, remove all the pins and re-pin the fabric to the frame so that the outline is the right way round.

Alternatively, you can use small pieces of double-sided tape to keep the original design next to the silk while you trace it so that you do not have to unpin and turn the silk over. If you decide to do this, do not attach your original drawing to the work surface, but cut small pieces of double-sided tape and place them along the edges of your drawing. Peel off the back of the tape and, with your frame silk side down on the work surface, place the drawing with the tape towards the silk until it sticks, temporarily, to the fabric. Turn over the frame and trace your design, which will show clearly even through a heavier silk. Remember to remove the original drawing before you apply the gutta or your silk will stick to the drawing paper when the gutta penetrates the fabric.

The outlines in my painting were drawn in silver gutta, and I used a medium-sized nib, making sure that the line was sufficiently thick to avoid bleeding. I tested this with a little water.

I moistened the bottom part of the silk and started to paint that area first, trying to merge in blue, red and yellow to give a soft-edged effect. I worked in the rest of the colours, alternating warm and cool colours as far as possible. The dark blue areas in the upper part of the picture were overlaid several times so that the tone of the colour darkened sufficiently. It is always best to work from light to dark because dark tones cannot be altered easily.

The final painting is a simple, bright evocation of the shapes and colours I enjoy in the cathedral.

11   The cushions of habutai and antung silk
that are described in Chapter 4.

4

Designing and Painting Cushions

Designing and making cushions is enjoyable, and painted silk cushions make unusual and attractive gifts for special occasions as well as being delightful decorations in your own home. The four cushions described in this chapter were all designed to go with the same fabric, which had been used to upholster a settee. Habutai and antung silks were used, and the finished cushions are illustrated in colour photograph 11.

PREPARING THE DESIGN

There are several ways you can select a design. Fig. 40 shows four designs that were based on the same fabric. For the first design (top left) I chose a motif and drew a free-hand enlargement of it (Fig. 41) in dark waterproof pen on a piece of card measuring 15 × 15in (38 × 38cm). When you are making cushions it is a good idea to cut out pieces of paper or card this size for the designs so that you can be sure that the designs are the right proportions for the cushion size. A square 15 × 15in (38 × 38cm) will fit into a plywood cushion frame of which the inner dimensions are also 15 × 15in (38 × 38cm). You can place your design in the frame to see if it looks satisfactory. I have cut several cushion frames to the same dimensions as I always make cushions the same size, but you could cut your frames to any dimension you require and draw your designs accordingly.

I developed the second design in a totally different way. I took a photocopy of the fabric, which I folded to show the motif I intended to use (Fig. 42), and then enlarged the photocopy from A5 (8¼ × 5¾in/210 × 148mm) to A3 (16½ × 11⅔/420 × 297mm). The A3 design fitted easily into the 15 × 15in (38 × 38cm) frame. I was also able to cut up the photocopy and use it as a template instead of using more time-consuming enlarging methods such as grids.

Both designs were made up in antung silk with Orient Express paints.

Fig. 40   The designs based on upholstery fabric for, at the top, the two antung cushions and, below, the two habutai cushions.

The designs on the cushions with the white background of habutai silk are deliberately simpler and bolder, but they were developed from the same motifs as the other ones. The bottom left design in Fig. 40 is based on the leaf-like shape that features on the second antung cushion. Again, I developed it from the photocopy, using the pattern made by the leaf edges, and drawing it free-hand in a linear, stylized way.

The fourth design, bottom right in Fig. 40, is a section of the motif used in the first cushion. I enlarged a section of the design and drew it in outline.

Fig. 41 Checking the proportions and neatening a free-hand enlargement of the design for one of the antung cushions within the frame.

Fig. 42   The design for the other antung cushion, together with the original fabric and an enlarged photocopy.

PREPARING THE FRAME AND TRACING THE DESIGN

All the cushion frames were prepared in the same way. I cut pieces of silk measuring approximately 17 × 17in (44 × 44cm) to allow for seams, and stretched them over the frames as described in Chapter 1.

So that the design is visible through the silk, the silk has to be placed next to the drawing as described in Chapter 3. Cushion-weight silk is usually quite heavyweight and not as transparent as the very fine silk that is used for

54

12   One of the antung silk cushions, together with a piece of the fabric and the experiments to find suitable shades of paint.

pictures and cards. It helps, too, if the original design is outlined strongly in a dark colour so that it shows more clearly through the silk.

I placed double-sided tape along the edges of the card on which the design had been outlined, adding some tape to the centre in case the card pulled away from the silk. After attaching the design to the underside of the silk the design was traced in fabric pen. The card was eased away from the silk and I was ready to gutta.

APPLYING GUTTA

The antung cushions

I decided to use gold gutta for the antung cushions because it suited the design and colour scheme. The nozzle of the gutta nib sometimes clogs when gold gutta is used, but do not lose your patience – just rinse out the nib, check for air bubbles and, if that does not work, keep pushing a length of thin fuse wire down into the nib. Remember to blow out any excess water after rinsing

55

the nib, and test it on a piece of scrap paper or cloth before you proceed with your design. To apply the gutta, I used a narrow nib and worked from the centre outwards to avoid causing smudges.

When any moist substance, including gutta and paint, is applied to antung, the silk slackens in the frame. You will find that you will have to re-stretch it as you go along, because it can be irritating when the silk is not taut and the gutta nib sinks into the fabric. When all the gutta has been applied, check carefully for any breaks in the lines and then leave the silk until it is completely dry. Take the silk out of the frame and fix the gutta by ironing. You should place the fabric on a clean cloth with the gutta side down – that is, the gutta is away from the iron – and iron for three minutes on a medium heat. Do not use the steam facility on your iron.

After ironing, re-stretch the silk on the frames with the wrong side to the top so that the gold gutta faces the work surface but is separated from it by the thickness of the frame. Use a narrow nib and go over the whole design again, but this time using transparent gutta. This is an insurance against bleeding when you come to paint the cushion, and although it is rather tedious, it is well worth the effort. The transparent gutta can be washed out when the paints have been fixed. You should fix the gold gutta before you apply the transparent gutta because heat can cause the transparent gutta to become embedded in the gold, and it can be more difficult to remove.

Fig. 43 Using a paintbrush to apply transparent gutta to large areas of one of the habutai cushion designs.

The habutai cushions

I used a different approach when I came to apply gutta to the habutai cushions. I decided to mask off some areas of the designs with transparent gutta so that I could work on them later. I drew all the outlines in transparent gutta and then used a medium sized paintbrush to apply the gutta to the areas I wanted to resist the paint. The gutta nib enabled me to achieve a neat edge, while the paintbrush gave good covering power for the larger areas (Fig. 43). It is easier to apply transparent gutta if you place a piece of dark card on the work surface under the frame. The dark background will help you to see the gutta more easily. Remember to draw a gutta line around the whole design of each cushion to stop colour from one area bleeding into another. Use the edge of the frame as a guide for this, and it is a good idea to use a large nib because a thick line will create a stronger barrier. These lines will not show later as they will be covered by piping and seams. Leave the gutta to dry naturally for at least 24 hours.

PAINTING THE SILK

The antung cushions

Before painting any design that is intended to match a colour scheme or fabric, you will need to experiment with your paints. I used Orient Express paints on the antung cushions, and tested the colours by applying dots of paint to a scrap of silk in the following combinations: (1) turquoise blue; (2) turquoise blue and grey; (3) grey; (4) night blue; (5) night blue and grey; (6) night blue, turquoise blue and grey; (7) china blue; and (8) china blue and grey.

I ruled out night blue, turquoise blue and china blue unmixed because they were too strong. That left me with five colours in the blue/grey range.

Next I mixed and matched browns and oranges: (9) fawn; (10) tabac; (11) fawn and tabac; (12) mandarin and tabac; and (13) sienna. I found all the browns/oranges acceptable, which gave me a colour range of five colours, most of which were mixtures of one or two colours.

Finally, I tried blending the blue/greys and orange/browns.

I eventually painted the cushions using a range of tones of blue/grey/turquoise and brown/orange, occasionally merging or overlaying the blue and brown mixes. Because the creamy background complemented the colour scheme so well, I decided to leave a substantial part of the background uncoloured.

The habutai cushions

I used Deka paints for the cushions made of habutai because the designs included large areas of transparent gutta. Paints that are fixed by immersion in a bath of chemicals are not suitable for this type of design as the gutta will soften and the paint will bleed. Heat-fixable paints, on the other hand, are ideal for patterns such as these.

I experimented with colour in the same way as for the antung cushions, and this time chose to use mixtures of ultramarine, turquoise, azure and sienna, turquoise and white, and orange, sienna and ochre. The colours were rather strong to use unmixed, pure orange being especially overpowering.

I painted the design based on the leaf motif with a wide brush in a very random fashion, trying to work in a range of colours to create a good balance of tones. Some, but not all, of the colours were overlaid. Using paints in this way does cause paint to build up on the gutta, but you can mop this up with a tissue or a piece of cotton wool, and it does not, in any case, seem to affect the gutta's ability to resist paint.

I used the same range of colours to paint the other habutai design, but this time I blended the colours together more in the larger areas and, within the outlined gutta areas, used a medium sized brush to overlay paints. I used a fine brush to paint smaller areas with tones of a single colour.

All the cushions were left for at least 12 hours so that the paint was completely dry. I then fixed the paint by ironing the silk, on a non-steam setting, for three minutes, then washed out all the gutta and thoroughly dried, ironed and re-stretched the fabric ready to work on the backgrounds.

To finish the pattern of leaves on the first habutai cushion I used gold gutta to outline all the shapes of the original drawing. I painted inside some of the gutta shapes in the white areas, having first outlined them in transparent gutta on the back of the fabric to prevent bleeding. The completed design has blended and overlaid colours applied at random and even, flat colours in the smaller areas, which were painted after the gold gutta was applied.

I finished off the second habutai cushion by simply outlining the shapes in gold gutta because I felt that this design did not need any extra painting.

COLOURING THE PIPING

To pipe each cushion I prepared a length of fabric approximately 67in (170cm) long and 2in (5cm) wide. To achieve this length I had to piece bits of silk together, but the joins are not obvious because I used narrow piping cord.

When the two strips of antung and two strips of habutai were ready, I folded each one repeatedly until I had four folded pieces measuring about 4in (10cm). I took the antung strips and dipped each end in the paint that was left in the palette and dipped the middle in another of the colours I had used for the cushion (Fig. 44). This saved wasting any Orient Express paints. I repeated this with the habutai strips and the remaining Deka paints. If there is not enough left you can always mix some more paint in your palette. This is an easy but messy way of making a variegated piping which coordinates with your cushion. It is wise to wear rubber gloves.

I decided to add some gold Deka fabric paint to the habutai piping to brighten it up. After drying and iron fixing it, I laid the piping on a clean sheet of white paper. Then I used Deka gold paint to paint zigzags on the piping. When the gold paint dried I ironed it and made up the piping in the usual way. Intermittent dashes of gold are visible in the finished piping.

13   The completed habutai silk cushions.

Fig. 44   Dip strips of piping silk in the paint left over in your palette so that the colours coordinate with the colours of the cushions.

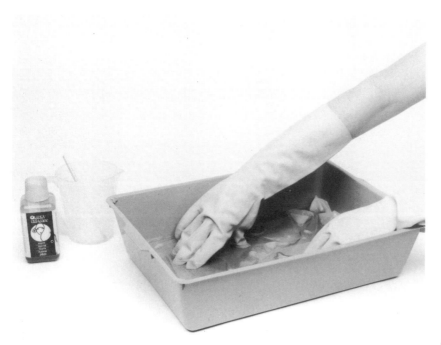

Fig. 45   A shallow plastic tray is ideal for holding the fixative for Orient Express paints.

FIXING THE CUSHIONS AND PIPING STRIPS

The antung cushions

The antung cushions and piping were fixed in the fixative recommended by Orient Express paints (Fig. 45). I used a shallow plastic tray, which I filled with 3½ pints (2 litres) of water at 68°F (20°C). I added four capfuls (approximately 2fl oz/50ml) of fixative and stirred it in. The cushion covers were fixed by being immersed individually in the fixative bath, stirred 10 times and left in the fixative for 5–10 minutes. When it was ready, I rinsed the silk thoroughly and allowed it to dry naturally. Both strips of antung piping were fixed in the same bath at the same time. I had to rinse them very thoroughly indeed as the silk absorbs a lot of paint when it soaks in a palette.

The habutai cushions

The habutai cushions and piping strips were left to become completely dry before I fixed the paint by ironing for three minutes on a non-steam setting.

When all the paints were fixed, I applied piping cord and zips and made up each cushion. I always use white cushion pads for white silk as the white enhances the colour of the silk, but cream or white pads can be used with antung silk.

14   *Cut Hayfield* A landscape, machine
embroidered almost entirely in straight
stitch, on painted silk.

5 *Embroidery on Painted Silk Backgrounds*

Painting on silk can provide a wide variety of backgrounds for any type of hand or machine embroidery. From simple patterns painted on silk to quite complicated landscape backgrounds that involve the use of a combination of gutta resist, fabric paints and silk paints, the whole range of painted silk items can be enhanced by embroidery.

Machine embroidery is a most exciting medium in which to work as you can use your needle to 'draw' almost anything you like. You can move your work in any direction – backwards, forwards, across to the left or right – that you wish to create a host of different effects. And even though the technique requires practice to complete complicated pieces, beginners can achieve excellent results by using some basic stitches simply but effectively on painted backgrounds. When you are appliquéing complicated designs machine embroidery skills come into their own. Satin stitch can be applied freely around any shape and used to give a more artistic finish (see Chapter 8 for satin stitches around flower shapes).

If you want to combine machine embroidery with painting on silk, begin with projects that will allow you to develop your skills gradually before embarking on a complicated design or landscape. It is also wise to practise on remnants of fabric. There are some excellent books on machine embroidery, and these go into great detail about the techniques. They are listed at the end of the book. Here, there is room only to cover the basic techniques and the preparation of the backgrounds.

BACKGROUNDS FOR MACHINE EMBROIDERY
First, always choose a medium or heavyweight silk; lightweight silk will tear when it is layered with stitching.

You should always leave enough fabric around the edge of the frame or hoop so that you can adjust it if necessary. Cut your silk so that it is about

1½in (4cm) wider than the frame; this will allow you to staple it to the frame with a comfortable overlap. Alternatively, you can economize by stitching strips of unwanted fabric to the edges of the silk and stapling these to the frame. Obviously you will need less silk if you do this.

Do not be tempted to staple silk to your frame before you have painted it. You must pin it first, then paint it and, when the background is complete and dry, staple it ready for stitching. Moisture causes silk to become slack, and when I first began painting backgrounds I wasted a lot of time removing staples and then stapling again. It is essential that silk for machine embroidery is absolutely taut, so using a hoop can be an advantage because you need no pins or staples but simply tighten up the ring. Nevertheless, I tend to use a wooden frame and to staple the silk to the frame because it will not slacken when it is stapled properly.

USING A HOOP FOR MACHINE EMBROIDERY

The fabric must be taut inside the hoop and the machine set up for embroidery. This will enable you to machine around, or add detail to, any type of shape or design, no matter how complicated it is.

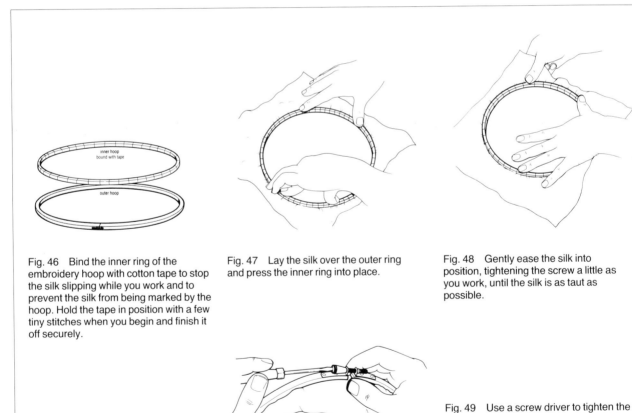

Fig. 46   Bind the inner ring of the embroidery hoop with cotton tape to stop the silk slipping while you work and to prevent the silk from being marked by the hoop. Hold the tape in position with a few tiny stitches when you begin and finish it off securely.

Fig. 47   Lay the silk over the outer ring and press the inner ring into place.

Fig. 48   Gently ease the silk into position, tightening the screw a little as you work, until the silk is as taut as possible.

Fig. 49   Use a screw driver to tighten the screw on the outer ring so that the silk is held as firmly and tautly as possible.

First, bind the inner ring of the hoop with cotton tape to stop the fabric slipping and the silk from being marked (Fig. 46). Lay the silk on the outer ring and press down the inner ring. (Fig. 47). Adjust the material by gently pulling it into position and gradually tightening the screw (Fig. 48). Tighten the screw as much as you can with a screw driver (Fig. 49)

USING A WOODEN FRAME FOR MACHINE EMBROIDERY

Lay the background fabric on your work surface and position the frame to accommodate the fabric (Fig. 50). Firmly pull the fabric over each corner and staple it in position (Fig. 51). Next, pull the fabric in the centre of each side of the frame and staple it down (Fig. 52). Continue to add staples all round the edge until the silk is completely stapled and absolutely taut (Fig. 53). Finally, cover the staples with tape to avoid scratching or snagging (Fig. 54).

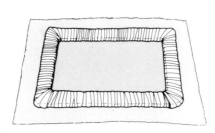

Fig. 50 Position the frame over the silk, having bound the frame with cotton tape.

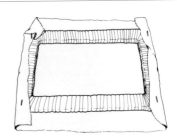

Fig. 51 Pull the silk over each corner, keeping it straight as you work, and staple it in position.

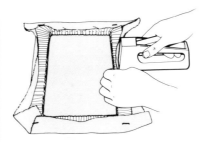

Fig. 52 Staple the silk in the centre of each side of the frame.

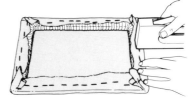

Fig. 53 Insert staples all around the frame so that the tension exerted on the silk is evenly distributed.

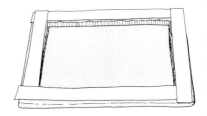

Fig. 54 Cover the staples with masking tape so that they cannot scratch or snag.

ADJUSTING YOUR MACHINE

Every sewing machine is different when it comes to embroidery, but you will need a good machine that is suitable for embroidery and robust enough for this type of work. Experiment with your machine to see what it is capable of. It is not necessary to have a complicated electronic machine – I only ever use straight stitch and zigzag for my work, and I know this is the case with several textile artists. Read the manual and learn which parts are which so that you can adjust your machine correctly; the basic parts are illustrated in Fig. 55.

Although your machine might differ slightly in some respects, follow the steps outlined here for embroidering with a machine.

First, lower the feed dog or cover it with the cover plate and turn the stitch indicator to the required stitch. Turn the stitch length to 0. When you use the free embroidery facility, the stitch length is controlled by the speed with which you move the hoop.

Fig. 55   The main parts of a sewing machine.

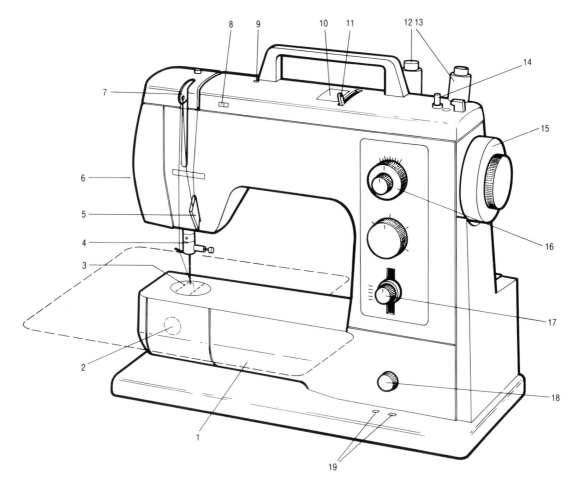

1 removable table   2 bobbin case (inside machine)   3 feed dog

4 foot attachment device   5 thread regulator   6 presser bar (at back of machine)   7 thread take-up lever   8 thread tension indicator

9 tension adjuster   10 stitch range (zigzag etc)   11 stitch selection lever   12 reel holder   13 reel holder   14 bobbin spindle

15 hand wheel   16 stitch width knob   17 stitch length knob   18 sewing/darning/embroidery knob   19 symbols for sewing/darning/embroidery

Unless I am using whipped stitch, I always adjust the top and bottom tension so that they are slightly looser than normal, but you may find that this is not necessary on your machine, so do not do it unless you need to. If you do not have a numbered lower tension on your machine be careful when you adjust the bottom tension as some bobbin cases can cause problems. I once unscrewed the bobbin screw too far, and it fell out and disappeared through a floorboard. Thread up your machine. I find that any good quality threads are suitable, and I rarely have problems that cannot be overcome by re-threading or re-setting the machine. If you have a free-arm machine, fit the removable table for extra support.

Place the hoop or frame with the taut fabric under the needle (Fig. 56). If you are using an embroidery foot, you may need to remove it before you can position the frame under the needle and replace it when the frame is in the correct place. Beginners should use an embroidery foot but, whether or not you are using a foot, you must remember to lower the presser foot lever or presser bar. This is absolutely vital; if you fail to do this, the threads will clog up the machine because the tension will not engage.

Hold the top thread to give it some tension and gently turn the hand wheel towards you to bring up the bobbin thread. Lower the needle – size 80 or 90 (11 or 14) is suitable – into the fabric and begin to stitch at a moderate speed. Hold the top and bottom threads with your left hand and control the frame with your right hand while you do this. You can cut the threads away when you have secured them with a few initial stitches. Continue to sew, guiding the frame or hoop with both hands. You can move from one area of your design to another without cutting off the threads each time, but remember to trim and fasten them off if necessary later. Whenever you change your cotton, top or bottom, raise and lower the presser foot lever so that you re-engage the top tension. Test that it is engaged by pulling the thread through the needle; if it runs loosely, the tension has not engaged.

Do not be put off if this appears to be complicated. Try re-adjusting your machine if things do not seem to be going well, and do several test pieces on scraps of spare material. As you get to know your machine's capabilities and gain experience of working with it, you will come to know how to handle almost every problem that arises.

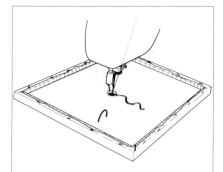

Fig. 56   If you are using an embroidery foot, you may have to remove it before you can position the hoop or frame under the needle. Remember that the silk in the hoop must be as taut as possible before you begin to embroider.

MACHINE EMBROIDERY STITCHES

The examples of machine embroidery illustrated in Fig. 57 cover a wide range of basic skills that can be applied to all types of work – decorating a painted piece of silk or machining a landscape. For reasons of space, the exercises were worked on one frame. However, if you wish to try them all, you should attempt each exercise on a separate frame or hoop.

Straight stitch

Sewing around shapes is a useful exercise for developing your control of the machine. It also helps to improve your accuracy. To work this exercise (seen

Fig. 57   Exercises in machine embroidery.

at top left of Fig. 57), prepare a simple patterned background. I used a wide gutta nib, which gives a very clear line, and blue, red and yellow Deka paints. I fixed the colours and washed out the gutta, and then I sewed around the shapes in dark blue and added some pattern inside them. If you want to add detail, use a fabric pen to draw in the lines and follow them with your needle. This type of background could be used on a sweatshirt or made into a card, so your exercises need not be wasted.

Colour photograph 14 shows a landscape by textile artist Alison Holt that was worked almost exclusively in straight stitch. It is, as you can see, a most versatile stitch and has been used to create textures ranging from leafy undergrowth to hay stubble.

Zigzag

Prepare a simple background for zigzag stitch. In this case I painted a block of four squares divided by gutta lines (Fig. 57, top right). There are four useful zigzag effects in this exercise. Set the machine for zigzag and use the machine in exactly the same way as for straight stitch. The first example, top left, shows how, when it is worked vertically, zigzag can be used to build up texture and tone. Here the frame was moved slowly at the bottom and more quickly at the top so that the stitches opened up gradually.

The second exercise, top right, shows zigzag worked horizontally, and the layers of stitches have been overlaid several times so that they provide a tonal development from dark to light.

The exercise in the bottom left-hand square shows zigzag tapering to a point, with the stitch width graduating from 0 to 4. Set the dial or stitch regulator (Fig. 58) on the highest number and begin sewing. Gradually turn the dial indicating the stitch width from 4 through all gradations to 0. This will cause the stitch to diminish gradually to a point. With practice you will be able to move the dial while the needle is moving and develop a flowing movement. If you wish, in addition to tapering lines of different thicknesses, you can move the stitch width regulator from 0 to maximum and back again to create a leaf or petal shape. Beginners may find it difficult to create evenly tapered lines at first because not only has the dial for stitch width to be altered manually, but at the same time the stitch length has to be controlled carefully and the direction of the line plotted accurately. This is why exercises are useful as they help to build up confidence and skill.

If you do find it difficult to alter the stitch width while the needle is moving, do it more slowly by bringing the needle up until it is just above the fabric and altering the stitch width dial while the needle is correctly positioned but out of the bobbin area. You can then continue to sew and the stitch can be altered in this way each time by bringing the needle up and keeping it in the same position in relation to the previous stitch.

The final zigzag exercise shows stitches created by curved movements of the hoop. Here the zigzag is stretched out and a staggered line created. All these stitches are extremely useful for landscape or pictorial work that requires texture, tone and pattern.

Fig. 58   The stitch width selector, with settings from 0 to 4.

Satin stitch

Satin stitch is a most useful stitch for machine embroiderers. It can be used for appliqué, landscapes and decorative stitching to name but a few. It is created by using a zigzag setting, moving the hoop or frame slowly and, at the same time, putting quite a lot of pressure on the foot pedal. The balance of foot pressure and the slow movement of the hoop comes with practice.

The four satin stitch exercises can be seen at centre left of Fig. 57. The first of them shows a painted background with satin stitch worked in various thicknesses. These lines of stitching can be easily worked by using the ordinary sewing mechanism, but when you are sewing around complicated shapes you will create a successful effect only if the flowing lines of machine embroidery are employed. The embroidery mechanism allows you to stitch virtually any shape. The width of the stitch is controlled by the dial on the machine, but the distance between stitches and their length is controlled by the movement of the hoop. A slow movement of the hoop causes the zigzag stitches to cram close together, creating a 'satin' effect. A rapid movement of the hoop creates less dense stitches and gives a more open zigzag.

The second example shows satin stitch tapering to a point, and this is achieved in a similar way to tapering zigzag stitches. The wheel has to be adjusted gradually through each size of stitch from 4 to 3½ to 3 to right down to 0 or from 0 to 4. This stitch can also be used to create leaf or petal shapes in a similar way to zigzag stitch.

In the third exercise (shown in the bottom left-hand square), whipped satin stich was used. To achieve this, the bottom thread was brought up to the top so that two colours, the top colour and the bobbin colour, show in the satin stitch. Whipped stitches of all types – satin or straight – are created by tightening the top tension. (Tension is discussed in detail in the description of whipped straight stitch below.) In this exercise the whipped satin stitch is also tapered, which is ideal for showing tone in a tree trunk or fence, for example.

In the final example, whipped satin can be seen in curving lines of different thicknesses. This exercise is very good for developing stitch control, and the lines can be used to great decorative effect.

Satin stitch outlines

In this example, Fig. 57, centre right, a background design was painted using a gutta outline and the three primary colours. I used both wavy lines and zigzags. Try painting a simple design of a similar nature and outlining it in satin stitch of various thicknesses.

Whipped stitch

The group of exercises in the bottom left-hand corner of Fig. 57 is a selection of patterns worked in whipped straight stitch. This is my favourite stitch: it gives a rich texture that allows a more 'painterly' effect to be created. Colour photograph 15 shows *Snowdonian Landscape*, for which I used only whipped stitch.

If you follow these basic steps, whipped stitch should prove straightforward.

15 *Snowdonian Landscape* A landscape
embroidered exclusively in whipped stitch on
painted silk.

Set up your machine by tightening the top tension and by carefully slightly loosening the lower tension. If you have a bobbin case with a screw, adjust it very gently (Fig. 59). You might find it convenient to keep two bobbin cases so that you do not have to alter the whipped stitch one all the time.

If you wish, use an embroidery foot. Lower the feed dog and set the machine for running stitch; the stitch width and the stitch length should both be at 0. Place the frame under the needle, lower the presser bar and exert pressure on the foot pedal.

The alteration in tensions causes the lower thread to rise up and wrap itself around the top thread, and this gives a two-colour effect. You may find that you have to exercise considerable patience before you can work in whipped stitch. Most beginners find that their thread or needle breaks frequently, and their tensions need to be changed several times. However, as you get used to whipped stitch, this will happen less often. Experiment by moving your hoop quickly, then slowly – the effects you will achieve are very interesting.

The first exercise in the group in the bottom left-hand corner of Fig. 57 shows straight lines of whipped stitch worked by moving the hoop very slowly. The bobbin thread is more evident and wraps itself around the top thread quite densely. Below this are a few curved lines, also worked by moving the hoop slowly.

In the top right-hand example, the hoop was moved quickly so that the stitch length widens. You can see more of the top thread, but speckles of bobbin thread add interest. Tone was created by overlaying stitches at the top.

In the bottom left-hand square curving, branch-like shapes were worked, and the whipped stitch has created a pleasant texture.

In the bottom right-hand square, texture and tone were created by moving the hoop up and down in a rhythm to create a zigzag pattern. This is not as regular as when the machine is set for zigzag, and it is very useful for landscapes and grass.

A simple landscape

The final exercise illustrated in Fig. 57 is a simple landscape. The horizon line was drawn in with gutta before the background was painted. A dark tone was used on the horizon line, and the paint was diluted as it moved away from the horizon.

Whipped straight stitch was used to work the trees, and three shades of thread were used to create medium, light and dark tones. The fields were stitched with the machine set on zigzag with a high top tension so that the zigzag became whipped. The path was 'drawn' in whipped straight stitch, worked from side to side, and the fence was also worked in whipped straight stitch. The tree in the foreground was stitched in tapering satin stitch with straight stitch leaves.

If you have worked through all the exercises shown in Fig. 57, you should now be able to design a small landscape or picture of your own that incorporates all or most of the stitches that have been described.

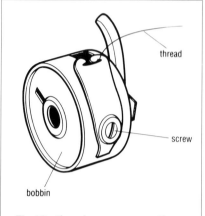

Fig. 59 If you have a screw on the bobbin case of your machine, adjust it slightly to loosen the tension.

CHOOSING A PICTURE AND PREPARING THE BACKGROUND

When you have selected a suitable piece of source material, your first task will be to consider its size and proportion in relation to the frame you will be using.

You may, for example, want to work from a picture that is smaller than the frame, and you could gutta around the image area of the photograph or sketch and use the spare background for practising stitches or testing colours, which can be very useful.

If your chosen picture is very small, enlarge it (using a diagonal grid as described in Chapter 3 or a photocopier). Not until you are happy with the dimensions of your final piece and have found a suitably sized frame can you begin to prepare the background.

If your image is relatively simple, you can draw a free-hand outline of it on to the silk using a fabric pen, simplifying the basic elements of the illustration and blocking in the areas you intend to paint. More complicated backgrounds require more planning and careful thought. In my first attempts to prepare backgrounds I made mistakes and tried to wash out the gutta lines and start again. Unfortunately, this did not work. Although the original lines appeared to wash out, they would show up when I painted over them. It is better to prepare carefully and to avoid mistakes. If you do make a mistake, use a fresh piece of silk for your second attempt. The discarded silk can be used for appliqué or for practising embroidery stitches.

Colour photograph 16 shows an embroidery of Monet's garden for which I used both fabric and silk paints and embroidered it almost entirely in whipped stitch. My source material was a series of photographs of a glorious tree in the gardens at Giverny. (Sadly, as I found on a recent visit, the tree has not thrived.) I altered the proportions slightly, leaving out part of the house and garden and making the sky area larger in the outline to be traced (Fig. 60). It is often difficult to decide which elements to outline, and in this picture, as usual, I decided to keep the basic background shapes as simple as possible. If you allow your outlines to become too complicated, you may find that the intrusive background competes with the stitching rather than contributing to a complementary balance of colour and design.

PAINTING AND EMBROIDERING A LANDSCAPE

Fig. 61 illustrates the stages of painting and embroidering the picture of Monet's garden.

First, I used a fabric pen to trace the outline I had prepared on to the silk. Then I drew all the lines with transparent gutta. The top left illustration in Fig. 61 shows the gutta outline and the completed painting. I usually paint the silk with silk paints first and then add fabric paint to areas that I want to make more substantial. Here, for example, I used Deka permanent paint to add detail to the house and to the path.

16 *Monet's Garden at Giverny* Both fabric and silk paints were used for the background, while machine embroidery was used for the detail.

The background should be painted in a fairly loose style, with the colours applied to give an impression of the scene. Aim to use colours that reflect the original source material as accurately as possible as they will form a basis for your stitching, and you may want to leave areas of painted background – a house or path or an area of shrubbery with no definite form, for example – free of stitching so that they will form part of the composition in their own right.

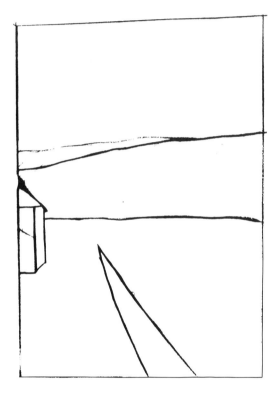

Fig. 60 The source material for *Monet's Garden at Giverny*, which is illustrated in colour photograph 16. Also shown here is the tracing for the background that I painted on the silk.

In the second stage, which can be seen at top right of Fig. 61, I have begun the machine embroidery by blocking in the hills in different tones of ochre and cream, using a horizontal whipped stitch to create texture. Next, I used a fabric pen to mark in the position of the trees and stitched them in whipped stitch too. Here, I used blue on the bobbin and green on top, which gave the bluish-green of the trees. Then I mapped in the dark shadows under the branches of the tree over the hills and drew in the dark brown/red branches with yellowy green foliage next to the house. The border of the path was 'drawn' in whipped stitches worked in a zigzag motion. Finally, I blocked in more of the basic dark tones in the foreground where shadows and dark undergrowth appeared.

75

The process was continued (Fig. 61, below left), but this time the main features of the tree were blocked in using whipped satin stitch to add tone to the branches. The basic lines of the tree were drawn in with fabric pen, although you can use tracing-paper if necessary. It would be possible to draw the tree very accurately on a piece of tracing-paper, place it in position and stitch the outline of the tree in straight stitch.

The paper can then be torn away and the details can be added in satin stitch. As you gain confidence, however, you will be able to use satin stitch directly on the background.

The penultimate stage (Fig. 61, below right), shows more detail added to the tree. This was done by building up layers of light tone over dark to give an impression of depth. It is important not to obscure all the background so that there can be an interplay of colour and texture between the stitching and the background. A wide selection of shades of turquoise, green, yellow and mustard, as well as pinks, was used on the tree, and you will need as wide a range as possible of colours that relate to your chosen subject.

After putting in the leaf and flower detail on the tree, I blocked in foreground foliage detail in a similar way. As you use your machine you can move across the picture in any direction to add detail, snipping off the joining threads later. You should always cut away excess threads at the back of your work to avoid dense layers of thread building up, because these are difficult to sew through.

The final picture (colour photograph 16) shows the completed shadow on the path and all the finer details.

The whole process of working in machine embroidery on a landscape is rather like building up an oil or acrylic painting. You work in layers of colour, placing light against dark and always attempting to let the background colours of the silk paints shimmer through to enhance the texture created by the stitching.

Painting skies

In the picture of Monet's garden I wanted a simple expanse of bright blue summer sky, so I used a light blue mix, working from the horizon line, diluting the paint to create a slight change of tone from the horizon upwards. A similar type of sky can be seen in *Snowdonian Landscape* (colour photograph 15), but I added a touch of lilac to enhance it.

In Alison Holt's picture of a hayfield (colour photograph 14) you can see a billowy cloud with a definite edge, which contrasts quite sharply with the blue area of sky. Here, the clouds were marked out with transparent gutta to retain areas of white. After the blue area had been painted and fixed, the gutta was washed out and the sky was ready for stitching. Complicated sky effects can be achieved in this way, using overlays of colour and blocking out with gutta at different stages.

If you prefer, you could paint cloudy or stormy skies free-hand, as was done in colour photograph 1. The more skill and experience you glean from practice, the more painterly your results will be.

Fig. 61   The main stages in painting and embroidering *Monet's Garden at Giverny*.

17 Six different backgrounds for use with hand stitching.

BACKGROUNDS FOR HAND EMBROIDERY

Colour photograph 17 shows six different backgrounds that have been used for hand stitching. For economy of space these different stitches and backgrounds were worked on one piece of silk, but you will find it easier to work them on individual pieces of fabric.

18   An unusual combination – handmade paper and painted silk.

Fig. 62   Running stitch. Take your needle in and out of the fabric to make rows or patterns of evenly sized and evenly spaced stitches.

Sprayed background with running stitch

In the example shown at top left, several spiral motifs were cut out of transparent sticky-backed plastic and, after masking off the rest of the silk, I sprayed with yellow, red and blue fabric paints to create an overlay of colour (see Chapter 6 for spraying). When the paint was dry, I applied running stitch in blue, red and yellow (Fig. 62). This exercise can be developed in many ways and it is the sort of design and stitch that works well when it is quilted.

Painted background with gutta outline using long and short stitch, French knots, split stitch and straight stitch

In the second example shown in colour photograph 17 the leaf and flower shapes were drawn in with gutta. After fixing the silk paint and washing away the gutta, I used long and short stitch (Fig. 63) to add detail to the petals, French knots (Fig. 64) for the flower centres, split stitch (Fig. 65) and straight stitch (Fig. 66) to edge the petals and add detail and edging to the leaves.

The background silk paint shows through and complements the stitching. Some of the shapes have been left unworked so that the effect of the stitching in combination with the paint can be seen more clearly. When you work in this way you will find that it is possible to disguise bleeding by stitching over it.

Salt effect background with French knots

In the third example the background was painted diagonally with primary colours, but salt crystals were applied in lines so that the colours were merged into each other as they were absorbed by the crystals (see Chapter 7 for salt effects). After washing and fixing, I worked some French knots using threads of different thicknesses. The knobbly texture of the knots goes well with the texture of the background.

Painted and textured fabric with fabric paint drawn with a gutta nib

The fourth background in colour photograph 17 was interesting to do because it employed a wide range of techniques. First, I painted the silk with pastel yellow, blue and pink, adding salt to create texture. I used a piece of cut paper to spray gold paint over the surface, and when this was dry, I added some stronger colour to parts of the design. Finally, I picked out areas of the design with blue fabric paint using a narrow gutta nib. When the paint was thoroughly dry, I fixed the whole design by ironing and then ironed a piece of Bondaweb to it. I cut out the part of the design I wanted, peeled off the backing paper and ironed the silk to the background.

I used seeding and straight stitch (Fig. 66) to pick out details of the design and to add texture and colour to some areas.

Free-hand painting with fly stitch

I painted this example entirely free-hand, applying the paint in a loosely symmetrical pattern. I painted yellow first, adding red and blue over the top.

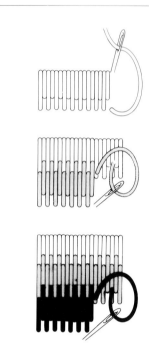

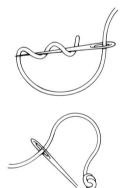

Fig. 63   Long and short stitch. Make a first row of alternately long and short stitches. Then work the following rows with stitches of similar length, merging these stitches with those of the preceding row.

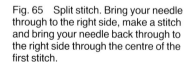

Fig. 65   Split stitch. Bring your needle through to the right side, make a stitch and bring your needle back through to the right side through the centre of the first stitch.

Fig. 64   French knots. Bring your needle through to the right side. Wrap the yarn two or three times around your needle, draw the needle through the knot so formed and then stitch back through the fabric, close to your starting point.

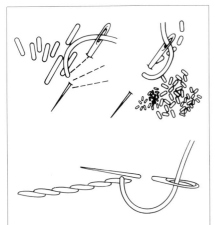

Fig. 66   Straight stitch, seeding and stem stitch. Straight stitches can be worked at random or evenly, and the stitches can vary in length. Seeding is really a random group of tiny running stitches, and you can emphasize them by going over each stitch twice. The stitch is used to fill areas with the appearance of scattered dots. With stem stitch make a straight stitch at the required angle. Bring the needle through on the left of the stitch, about two thirds along it. Keeping the thread to the right, make a second overlapping stitch of the same length.

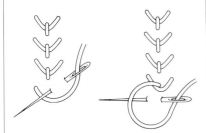

Fig. 67   Fly stitch. Make a loose stitch on the front of your fabric and hold it in a V-shape with a tiny running stitch. Fly stitch can be worked horizontally or vertically, and you can make a continuous line by lengthening the holding stitch.

As the silk paint dried, the colours merged. I chose fly stitch (Fig. 67) because it seemed to work well with the symmetrical nature of the design. This sort of design could be worked just as effectively in repeats and to a different scale.

Landscape with assorted stitches

The last example in colour photograph 17 is a simple landscape that was drawn in with gutta. I based the picture on a photograph I had taken but drew the design free-hand, simplifying the basic outline. I drew cow parsley outlines, horizon line trees and foreground foliage in gutta and then painted the whole the thing with silk paint. After fixing the paint and removing the gutta, I stitched in the trees on the horizon line using a mixture of long and short stitch and straight stitch. I used stem stitch to work the horizon line and the stems and branches of the foreground plants. The detail on the umbels was worked in fly stitch and French knots, the foreground leaves were worked in split stitch, long and short stitch and chain stitch (Fig. 68), and I left part of the foreground unworked so that the effects of the stitches and the linear nature of the gutta lines may be seen. The field behind the foreground plants works well without stitching, although more could be added if desired.

These simple backgrounds could form the basis of a wide range of different projects for hand sewers as they offer starting points for abstract and figurative work of all types. Hand sewing can, of course, also be combined with machine stitching to great effect.

MIXED MEDIA WORK ON SILK

Colour photograph 18 shows an unusual combination of silk and handmade paper. Mary Neukom's work was developed from a study of the columns in the façade of the Natural History Museum, London. The paper, which was made from nettles, provides the basis for machine embroidered metallic thread work. Tiny gold beads were added, and coloured paper motifs taken from the patterns in the columns of the museum were stitched on top of the metallic thread and paper base. In the centre of the work, four sections were loosely faggoted together. All the paper pieces were laid on a rich silk background, which was painted in the same colours used to colour the paper. The lustre of the silk is a perfect base for the richly worked, textured paper.

Fig. 68   Chain stitch. Bring the needle and thread through from underneath the fabric, anchor the thread with the thumb of your left hand and place the needle back in the original hole. Bring the needle back through the fabric, beneath the hole, according to the length of stitch required, making sure the thread is under the needle before pulling the needle and thread through gently to make a chain. Repeat.

6

Spraying

Spraying is an enjoyable and effective way of working on silk. The equipment you will need can be anything from a sophisticated airbrush, which is used with a compressor, to a simple mouth diffuser, which you blow through yourself.

Both airbrushes and mouth diffusers are usually used with masks and stencils to create a range of background shapes and images. Masks, as the name suggests, are used to protect part of an image while the area outside the mask is sprayed. For example, if you hold a piece of torn paper against a background and spray lightly, you will get a soft, ragged effect at the edge of the mask. When stencils are used, paint is sprayed or painted on to the shapes cut out of the stencil. For example, if you cut a series of circles out of a piece of paper and attach the paper to the silk, when you spray, the circles will be filled with colour while the rest of the silk will remain uncoloured.

Stencils and masks can be used in conjunction. They can be as simple as a doily or a scrap of torn paper, or complicated stencils and masks can be made and used to give complex and subtle overlays of colour. As long as you follow the right procedure, however, the results will always be highly effective.

It is best to experiment with different masking effects and paints before embarking on a specific design involving spray technique. Fig. 69 shows several different examples, all of which can be used as backgrounds for embroidery and made into little cards or pictures. All were done with a mouth diffuser. I worked all of them on one piece of silk, masking off each section as I went along, but you can, of course, do each one separately, in which case you should leave a border for mounting in a card or frame.

Two types of mouth diffuser are available (Fig. 70). I prefer the kind that have a fixed aperture of 90° simply because they are easier to use. Whatever kind of mouth spray you use, you have to keep the angle at 90° or the paint or dye will not come out. This kind of diffuser also has a plastic mouthpiece, which can be detached and washed. The other kind has an adjustable

19 *Origami* A wall hanging inspired by Japanese origami paper and executed on silk in painted and sprayed fabric and silk paints with gutta.

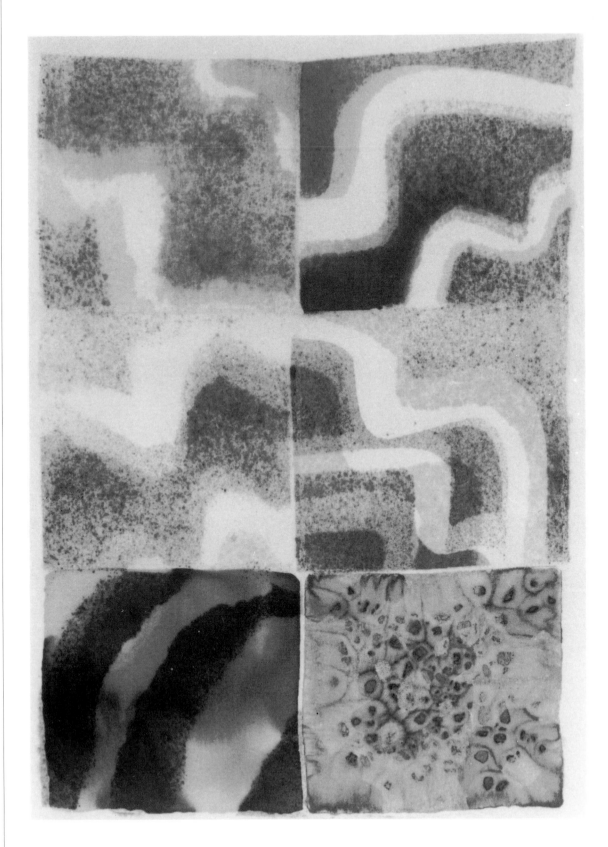

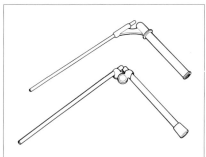

Fig. 69 Some of the effects that can be achieved by spraying.

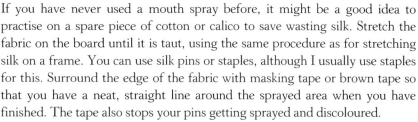

Fig. 70 Mouth diffusers. The spray at the top has a fixed aperture and a removable mouthpiece. The lower kind has an adjustable aperture.

aperture, and you have to think about keeping the angle steady at 90° as well as guiding paint and blowing.

You will also need the following equipment before you can begin to spray:
– a board on which to stretch the silk
– some sheets of blotting-paper
– a piece of the transparent sticky-backed plastic of the kind that is used to protect books and pictures
– double-sided or masking tape
– fabric and silk paints
– a staple gun or silk pins.

PREPARING TO SPRAY

If you have never used a mouth spray before, it might be a good idea to practise on a spare piece of cotton or calico to save wasting silk. Stretch the fabric on the board until it is taut, using the same procedure as for stretching silk on a frame. You can use silk pins or staples, although I usually use staples for this. Surround the edge of the fabric with masking tape or brown tape so that you have a neat, straight line around the sprayed area when you have finished. The tape also stops your pins getting sprayed and discoloured.

Cover your table or working surface with newspaper. If you can lean your board against a wall, make sure that the wall is covered with newspaper too. If you are working on a table, you will need an old chair or stool to lean your board against. It is a good idea to protect the chair with paper or an old sheet as the paint will not come off clothes and most other surfaces. Lean the board against the chair or wall. If you wish place a heavy object in front of it to stop it sliding forwards – which could be disastrous if all the paints you were using were arrayed in front of the board!

When the board is in position, mask off the part of the fabric you are not spraying (Fig. 71). I usually cut a piece of paper to the same size as the background fabric and fold it into sections so that I can cut and fold each section to reveal the area to be sprayed. When an area is complete, the paper section can be re-attached to protect the completed area. However, if you are working in a single technique on one piece of fabric, you can, of course, dispense with this.

BLOTTING-PAPER MASKS

When I was spraying the top left-hand design in Fig. 69 I used torn strips of blotting-paper (which you can see in Fig. 71). Decide on the shape or pattern for your stencils, and either tear them free-hand or draw lines to follow when tearing or cutting. Torn edges leave interesting textured edges. Hold the strips of blotting-paper in position with double-sided tape or masking tape.

I used blue, red and yellow silk paint for this example, and began with yellow. To use the diffuser, place the longer end in the container of paint and point the aperture at a spot to the left of the area to be sprayed, aiming

initially at the newspaper behind your work. Start to spray from this spot, guiding the spray lightly across the edges of the blotting-paper mask. It is a sensible precaution to begin spraying away from the fabric because a concentration of paint tends to come out as you start to blow, and this can become a dark, unsightly blotch.

As you continue to blow, a steady spray of paint will build up, and by building up a flow before you move on to your fabric you can avoid unattractive blobs or concentrations of colour.

As soon as you complete the first spraying, blot the area you have sprayed. This prevents any excess paint from seeping under the blotting-paper mask. If you want to build up dark tones, you will need to apply several layers of light colours.

Blowing heavily in concentrated areas does not give subtle or attractive results, and the beauty of spraying is the subtle effect you can achieve with layers of colour.

When I was happy with the first spray, I moved the blotting-paper strips so that they masked off some of the yellow area and some of white. You should always aim to leave some background white to highlight the colours you create. Try to move the strips so that they are in sympathy with the shapes you have already created. Use new tape to attach them to the fabric if necessary.

Wash and dry your diffuser, then spray on the second colour; I used red in this example. Remember that different kinds of red create different secondary colours – crimson will give you a bluish-purple while scarlet gives a brownish-purple. Spray the second colour as before, blotting the paint as soon as you have finished.

Again, wash and dry the diffuser, then gently move the blotting-paper masks. This time I kept some pure yellow, some pure red and white masked off. Spray the final colour (I used blue), blot and remove the paper masks. If you use the colours I did, you will have a simple but attractive linear pattern in which blue, red and yellow have mingled to create secondaries.

This simple idea can be used to create many different patterns and sequences, and the process can be used for any type of design. Remember that silk paints flow easily out of the spray and do not need to be blown hard. Gentle control is important.

TRANSPARENT PLASTIC MASKS

Sticky-backed transparent plastic is extremely useful for masking, and it is available in wide rolls for large work. You can trace shapes through it, cut them out accurately, peel off the adhesive backing paper and attach the stencil or mask to the surface to be sprayed. I used simple wavy lines cut from the plastic for the top right-hand design in Fig. 69, and, as you can see, they give a much crisper line than blotting-paper strips.

I used exactly the same procedure and colours as with the previous example, but because the plastic is adhesive, no tape is required.

Fig. 71 Before you begin, mask the area of the fabric you do not want to spray. When I was working on the backgrounds shown in Fig. 69, I folded a sheet of paper into six so that I could cut and fold it as necessary to reveal the area I wanted to spray. You can see the strips of blotting-paper, held in position with masking tape, that I used to create the pattern shown in the top left-hand corner of Fig. 69.

SPRAYING WITH FABRIC PAINTS

I used fabric paints to complete the two examples in the centre of Fig. 69. The left-hand design was sprayed over blotting-paper masks, while transparent plastic masks were used for the right-hand pattern. I generally use Deka fabric paints for spraying, but they have to be diluted with water. The proportions of two-thirds paint to one-third water usually work, although some adjustment may be necessary. Like Deka silk paints, fabric paints are fixed by ironing.

If you want pale tones remember to add colour to white, rather than white to colour. You will also need several little jars to mix the paints in.

USING SILK AND FABRIC PAINTS TOGETHER

The bottom left-hand example in Fig. 69 shows a background painted with yellow and red Deka silk paints, which were oversprayed with blue Deka permanent fabric paint. This exercise has a lot of potential for different designs. As both the silk and the fabric paints are fixed by ironing, they make an ideal combination.

COMBINING A SALT EFFECT WITH SPRAYING

The last design in Fig. 69 shows a salt-effect background that was sprayed with Deka white fabric paint (see Chapter 7 for using salt). The effect of the fabric paint, which was used with transparent plastic stencils, has been to create a pale pink tone with the texture showing through. You could work on this with gutta if you wanted. I used a paint that was not quite opaque, but you could choose an opaque paint if you preferred; Pebeo opaque paint does not allow the background to show through and is very useful for using on dark areas.

COMBINING SPRAYING WITH OTHER TECHNIQUES

Colour photograph 19 shows a wall hanging in which I employed several techniques, including spraying. The inspiration for the hanging was Japanese origami paper. Japanese design in whatever guise is always fascinating and inspiring, and I never tire of looking at the lacquer work and fantastic kimonos.

Preparing the design

I took several photographs of a selection of origami papers, which I arranged so that they overlapped to make the designs appear to blend into one each other. I chose the photographs that I considered to be most successful and enlarged them on a photocopier in black and white. In the end I chose to use three photocopies of two different photographs. I cut these down into oblongs of equal size and arranged them on a piece of cartridge paper, alternating the patterns and endeavouring to create an asymmetrical design within the rigid framework. I drew around the inner edge of my large frame so that I knew the dimensions within which I had to work. When I was happy that each segment of the design was well placed, I glued the six sections down (Fig. 72), taped the whole thing to my work surface and took a tracing using a dark blue pencil (Fig. 73).

Applying the gutta

I traced the outline of the whole design in transparent, water-soluble gutta using the narrowest size of nib. Then I outlined the oblongs with a larger nib because I wanted to make sure that paint did not bleed over the straight edges.

I next chose some shapes that I wanted to leave white, and used a small paintbrush to paint them in transparent gutta.

Applying the paint

When the gutta was completely dry I prepared my paints. Deka paints are best for this technique as they can be applied over quite large areas of gutta without affecting the gutta. I chose a very simple colour scheme – red, yellow,

Fig. 72   My layout of the photocopies of the origami paper, which formed the basis of the wall hanging shown in colour photograph 19.

Fig. 73   I used a dark blue pencil to trace the photocopies shown in Fig. 72.

orange, yellow-green and dark green. The dark green was made from equal measures of dark blue and green with just a dash of yellow.

I tried to create a balance of tones without painting all the oblongs in exactly the same way. In the wave-like shape that features in three of the segments, I moved from one colour through two more, blending each colour, but making the order of the colours different in each block. I painted some colours in a flat tone, while others merge from light to dark. In some areas one strong colour, such as red, merges directly with the strong dark green. I used a variety of painting methods.

Spraying areas of the silk

I took the silk from the frame and fixed the paint by ironing for three minutes. I then washed it in a bleach-free washing agent. When the silk was completely dry, I re-stretched it on the frame. I then used a ball-point pen to trace the areas I intended to spray on to a sheet of sticky-backed transparent plastic (shiny side up), working from the original outline drawing I had done

20   *Sea Lavender* A landscape on antung silk, with a background of sprayed silk paints and applied stitching.

with the blue pencil. If you make an error when you are using ball-point pen on adhesive plastic you can rub it out with some damp paper towel.

I cut out oblongs of transparent plastic that were larger than the oblongs in the picture, but I drew along the edges of the design using a ball-point pen and a ruler. These lines helped me to position the stencil on the background correctly. Next, I placed the stencils in position and used masking tape to mask off every part of the silk that was not covered. If you find that re-stretching the silk distorts the fabric and that the stencils are not quite accurate, you can stick some small bits of transparent plastic over the affected areas. You can alter the size of any area by adding strips of carefully cut plastic film, but even if your spray is not absolutely correctly positioned, you can always disguise anything you do not like when you go on to the next stage.

When I was satisfied that the stencils were in the right place, I sprayed the whole area, moving from left to right and spraying and blotting four layers of green fabric paint before I was happy with the strength of the colour. If you are not confident enough to spray the whole design at once, block off areas and spray a small part at a time. When I had finished spraying, I removed all the stencils and tape.

Drawing into the design

The next stage was to draw into the design using fabric paint. I used undiluted dark green fabric paint with a narrow gutta nib. I did not want to outline each area but just pick out a few parts of the design with the dark green. I decided that gold gutta would suit the design, so, using a narrow gutta nib, I picked out other areas with gold gutta. When this was completely dry, I decided to go around each shape with gold but using a slightly wider nib to give greater emphasis.

I drew into the background border with gold gutta, extending the lines of the design and adding lines to break up the white areas. Finally, I painted the background in tones of green that I shaded from light to dark, with a few areas of red to add contrast.

Making the wall hanging involved a combination of techniques and it took a while to complete, but all the techniques work well together and the colourful result was worth the effort. The method described here can be applied to any type of wall hanging. Working in units makes the procedure easier because the areas are distinctly defined and work on their own as well as together. It is essential to have an overall colour scheme if this sort of work is to succeed.

SPRAYING AND QUILTING

Fig. 74 shows a detail of a sprayed and quilted cushion. Simple spray designs can be given added interest by quilting, which can be done by hand or by machine. Machining is, of course, quicker, but both methods give attractive results.

Fig. 74   A detail from a sprayed and quilted cushion.

Spraying the background

I stretched a piece of silk, 17½ × 17½in (44.5 × 44.5cm) on a board and masked off an area measuring 15 × 15in (38 × 38cm). I taped over the pins to leave a neat edge.

I cut out a range of spiral shapes in transparent plastic, varying the sizes of the spirals and making some quite small and others comparatively large. I removed the backing paper and attached the spirals to the silk in a random design.

I sprayed yellow fabric paint first, blotting and spraying several layers. Then I moved the spiral shapes around, making sure that I kept some of both the white background and the pure yellow areas free from paint. The next colour I sprayed was red, and I followed the same procedure. Finally, I moved the spirals and sprayed with blue, which I applied quite strongly in places to give strength of tone to the design.

I removed the masking tape and plastic film, left the paint to dry overnight, carefully removed the pins and fixed the paints by ironing.

Quilting

Three layers of fabric are used in quilting, whether it is done by hand or by machine and the type of fabric varies according to the article being made.

First, cut a piece of wadding to fit the top layer. The actual process of quilting causes the fabrics to shrink, so you must remember to allow for this or you will end up with a smaller article than you originally intended. Although it is not a disaster if you are making something like a cushion, forgetting that the quilted fabric gets reduced in size would be a problem if you were making something like a bag.

Wadding comes in various weights and types. Polyester is versatile and easily available, but you can also buy cotton, wool and silk wadding. The weight will depend partly on personal preference and partly on the nature of the article to be made, but as a rule the thickness of the quilting will be about half the thickness of the original wadding. If you want an extra-thick article, you could use two layers of wadding.

Second, cut a piece of backing fabric to the required size. This can be muslin, cotton, calico or any similar material.

Pin three layers of fabric – the silk, the wadding and the backing – together through all thicknesses, inserting the pins from the centre outwards, along the diagonals. Tack the layers of fabric together, again working from the centre out, and using small stitches on top. If you use large stitches they will catch in the foot if you use a machine.

Machine quilting

The techniques of machine embroidery are discussed in detail in Chapter 5. Quilting by machine is relatively straightforward as long as you observe the following steps.

First, lower the feed dog and attach the darning foot. Then set your machine for running or straight stitch and place the fabric layers under the foot, remembering to lower the presser bar (Fig. 75). Bring up the bottom

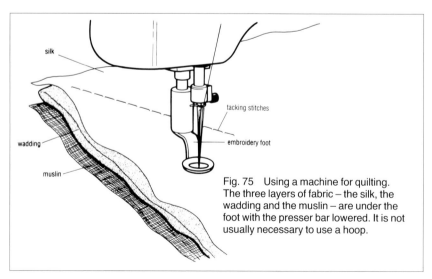

silk

tacking stitches

embroidery foot

wadding

muslin

Fig. 75   Using a machine for quilting. The three layers of fabric – the silk, the wadding and the muslin – are under the foot with the presser bar lowered. It is not usually necessary to use a hoop.

thread and check the tension. If the top thread runs loosely, raise and lower the presser bar a few times until the tension engages.

When I quilted the cushion cover illustrated in Fig. 74, I worked from the centre out, stitching around the spiral shapes with blue, red and yellow threads. I reset the machine for satin stitch (zigzag setting) and selected some spirals to stitch. These I sewed in graduated satin stitch – that is, the stitch narrowed at the end of the spiral. When I had finished the machining, I trimmed off all the loose ends, piped the cushion and finished it off with a backing piece.

Spraying is a technique that can be easily combined with quilting, and a cushion cover is a straightforward piece with which to start, although as soon as you have mastered the technique you will be able to undertake more complicated projects.

SPRAYED BACKGROUNDS FOR MACHINE EMBROIDERY

Colour photograph 20 shows a subtle and delightful machine embroidered landscape by textile artist Caryl Webb. She used Deka silk paints as a background for the work, and these were applied to the cream antung using an airbrush with a compressor. The principles for spraying with a compressor are the same as for spraying with a mouth diffuser – the silk must be stretched very taut on a frame, and stencils and masks are used to create the required shapes.

When you use an airbrush with a compressor you must take one or two precautions. First, because the power of the spray is considerably greater than that from a mouth diffuser, you should wear a face mask. Second, you should always spray in a well-ventilated area.

There are several types of airbrush available which offer varying levels of sophistication. Those at the top end of the range do give fine effects, but whatever kind you use, always be very careful about cleaning out the nozzle and mixing the paint or dye to a fine consistency. Imperfectly mixed paint or dye can cause blockages in the airbrush and result in nasty blobs on the silk. Practise using an airbrush with different stencils and masks using the approaches for mouth diffusers described earlier in this chapter. When you have mastered the basic techniques you can try your hand at figurative composition.

Spraying a background

Fig. 76 shows a frame, silk and stencil prepared for spraying a similar background to that used in *Sea Lavender*.

The first step was to take a paper tracing from the original drawing. As you can see, the different parts of the stencil remain attached to the body of stencil, which is stuck to the silk with double-sided tape.

The sky was sprayed first, using soft layers of Deka paint. Torn paper masks were used to create the soft-edged cloud effect. When the sky was finished, it was blocked out by folding back the paper stencil until it completely covered the sky area.

Next, the horizon line basic colours were sprayed on. Three different light tones were used to suggest the distance of the fields in this area. The three strips were alternately folded back and replaced after spraying. Sprayed paint dries very quickly, so once an area has been sprayed it can be masked off almost immediately, although you can use a hair-drier to speed up the process. Another advantage of spraying is that it rarely causes the silk to lose its tautness, so you can staple the silk before spraying and embroider it almost immediately. Occasionally, however, it will need to be re-stretched. Hand-painted silk backgrounds, on the other hand, must be pinned for painting and stapled when the silk is dry to ensure that the material is absolutely taut.

In order to spray the river, the cut mask was folded down to reveal the area for spraying (Fig. 77). The area was sprayed to create a gradual movement of

Fig. 76   A frame with a piece of stretched silk and a stencil in position, ready to be sprayed with an airbrush.

tone from dark to light and dark again at the edges of the river. The highlighted area in the centre adds brightness and interest. A flat tone here would have considerably lessened the vitality of the composition.

When the river was completed, the foreground land areas were sprayed on, and details were added with fabric paint. The shadows at the edge of the field were strengthened with fabric paint and some texture was added.

Finally, the machining was done. Lines of whipped stitch picked out the fields on the horizon. The distant trees were stitched using different tones of green, and the foreground detail was also worked in whipped stitch.

The machine embroidery textures and colours complement the sprayed background and create a fascinating blend of paint and stitchery. The sprayed mount, which is a feature of Caryl Webb's work, extends the picture by echoing the colours of the composition.

Fig. 77   Using an airbrush and a stencil to spray the river.

21   *Cyclamen* Textured silk used with
appliqué and whipped stitch.

Using Salt, Antifusant and Alcohol

SALT AND CRYSTAL EFFECTS

Very attractive patterns can be created on silk by using salt or dishwasher crystals. When they are sprinkled on to painted silk that is still moist, the salt or crystals absorb the paint, creating a bleached, textured effect on the silk. The scarf and box in Fig. 78 illustrate the results of this technique.

This textured silk is very useful for making scarves and for piping cushions, and textured fabric can be used for backgrounds in pictures or on cushions and for pieces to be used in appliqué. Not the least of the technique's uses is to cover mistakes in backgrounds; if there is a stain on a background, salt effects can be employed to cover it.

You will need rock salt or dishwasher crystals and fine salt for salt solutions. Fig. 79 illustrates some of the effects that can be achieved. All six examples were done with Deka paint. The top left-hand example shows simply the effects of randomly applied salt.

In the second example, salt was applied in rows on stripes of paint. As the salt pulls in the paint, attractive patterns appear along the edges of the stripes.

In the example at centre left, dishwasher crystals were applied at random, and the mottled effect seems exaggerated by the larger crystals. At centre right the crystals were arranged in circles.

In the example in the bottom left-hand corner, a saturated salt solution was prepared and transferred to the painted silk by means of a pipette.

The final example illustrates the combination of painted areas with salt-patterned areas. Gutta was used to prevent the salt from affecting the painted area, which can be completed before or after applying salt to the background.

Applying salt or crystals at random

You must stretch the piece of silk and raise the frame well clear of the surface of your table or working area. If you do not, the weight of the salt and paints will cause the silk to sink and touch the work surface, resulting in tidemarks.

Prepare the paints for application and make sure you have enough to cover the area of silk to be worked. I usually experiment on a small hoop first. Moisten the surface of the silk with a clean wet brush, but do not saturate it. Apply your paints at random but work as quickly as you can so that the paint does not begin to dry before the salt is added.

Drop the salt or dishwasher crystals on to the silk so that they are evenly spread out (Fig. 80). If you are using rock salt, it is worth drying it in the oven for a short period as it becomes more absorbent, but I have always used dishwasher crystals straight from the packet with no problems.

Fig. 78   A box in painted and textured silk and a scarf in textured silk.

Fig. 79   Some of the effects that can be achieved by the use of salt and dishwasher crystals.

22   Roses painted on silk, with salt used to create the appearance of blemishes on the petals.

23   Antifusant was used to help create the translucent appearance of the sweet pea petals.

Leave the frame, preferably overnight, to dry and then remove the crystals or rock salt, which should be kept in an airtight jar. You will notice that the crystals will have absorbed the dye and become pastel coloured. They can, nevertheless, be used several times.

Iron your silk or place it in a bath of fixative before using it in whichever way you intend.

Do not be deterred if your results are disappointing; there may be several reasons. If you place your frame next to a radiator or too close to a heat source, it may dry too soon. If you do not moisten the silk enough, the salt or crystal effect will be inhibited. If you apply too much moisture, on the other hand, it will drown the effect. As I have pointed out before, different paints work in different ways, and you should experiment until you find a way that works for you and your chosen paints.

If you want to cover a large area it is best to get a friend to help you apply the crystals as you apply the silk paint.

The picture of a cyclamen in colour photograph 21 is an example of the way in which textured silk can be used with an image. I worked from a sketch of a cyclamen and decided to use Orient Express paints in shades of pink and green. I prepared some pieces of habutai, using salt on some and dishwasher crystals on others, and ironed Bondaweb to all the pieces. After doing this, I selected those areas I thought resembled leaves or petals. Next I made templates of the cyclamen flowers and leaves and drew around them on the selected pieces with a fabric pen. I cut out each piece and arranged them all on a piece of white habutai, which I had stapled to an embroidery frame. The frame was sufficiently large for me to iron the pieces on to it, even though the silk was already stapled to the frame. I removed the backing paper of the

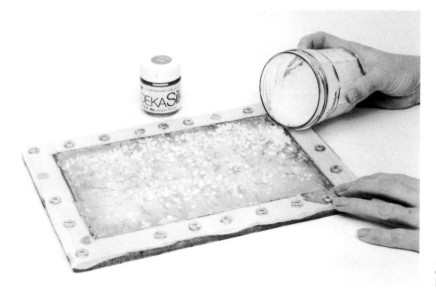

Fig. 80 Applying dishwasher crystals to a piece of painted silk. The crystals must be distributed evenly over the surface of the silk before the paint begins to dry.

Bondaweb and ironed through a thin cloth (baking parchment serves the same purpose), to keep the fabric clean and to prevent any Bondaweb adhesive ruining my iron. I decided to iron the pieces onto the stretched silk because I was afraid that if I ironed them on to a loose piece of silk and then stretched it, the pieces would distort before I could stitch around them.

Next I picked out details of leaf and petal patterns using whipped stitch. When I had finished the stitching, I cut a border of dark green silk, about ¾in (1.5cm) wide, to which I had attached some Bondaweb and, having removed the picture from its frame, ironed the green border on to the white silk to frame the cyclamen.

Finally, I cut out the outer pale pink and green border, measuring it carefully first so that it left enough dark green showing, and ironed it in place.

The silk used for the scarf in Fig. 78 is composed entirely of patterns created by the random application of crystals on a freely painted background, but the silk for the box uses the combination of crystal patterns with painted areas illustrated in Fig. 79 (bottom right). The lid of the box is made of habutai and the base of dupion silk. The flower design was drawn on the habutai with transparent gutta and the design painted in reds, oranges and greens. The surrounding area was painted with grey silk paint and dishwasher crystals were placed on the moistened silk. When they were dry, the crystals were removed from the silk and the whole piece fixed by ironing. The transparent gutta was washed out and finally the flower motif was embellished with silver gutta.

The dupion silk that was used for the base has an attractive texture of lines and nobbly areas. When it is painted, the colour catches on the nobbly parts and runs along the lines of the weave, creating an effect rather like Ikat weaving.

In colour photograph 22 I used salt to create the effect of a blemish on the petal of the rose. There are many ways of using salt to advantage for pictorial and patterned work.

Using salt or dishwasher crystals to form a pattern
To achieve the kind of effect illustrated in the centre right example of Fig. 79, you should carefully apply crystals with tweezers so that they create shapes where colours overlap. The salt or crystals will absorb each colour of paint, creating a colour mix – for example, red and yellow will create an orange texture.

Using a salt solution to create patterns
A salt solution can be used to create interesting patterns, similar to the one illustrated in the bottom left-hand corner of Fig. 79. A strong solution is most effective. I add salt to a jar or container three-quarters full of water until no more salt will dissolve. If a pipette is used to transfer the solution to a background moistened with silk paint, a pattern of pale tones in flowing shapes results. You can work into these with coloured gutta or fabric paint if you wish.

105

Using a salt solution to inhibit the spread of paint

A solution of salt can be used to inhibit silk paint if you want to paint free-hand without the paint spreading too much. The anemones appliquéd to the sweatshirt (see Chapter 8) were painted on a piece of silk that had been soaked in salt solution overnight. The next day I dried and ironed the silk, before painting on the anemones and adding details in fabric paint.

ANTIFUSANT

Antifusant is a transparent substance that can be painted on to those areas of the silk where you want to prevent the silk paint from spreading freely. The advantages of antifusant are that it can be applied selectively and it is controllable. It allows you to combine the free-flow effect of silk paint with highlighted areas so that highlighted areas are not swamped by paint, which can easily happen no matter how experienced you are.

When I was working on the sweet peas illustrated in colour photograph 23, I used antifusant on each petal before painting them to help create the transparent quality of the flowers. In the landscape with poplars in colour photograph 24, I painted the lightest area of the water with antifusant and the rest with a mixture of darker paints. The antifusant kept the light areas of water as light as possible without a harsh gutta line being necessary. Finally, I painted the light effects using Deka fabric paints in white and bluish-white.

ALCOHOL, METHYLATED SPIRITS AND WATER

Using pure alcohol, methylated spirits and water on dry painted silk creates interesting results. The liquids diffuse the silk paint, creating patches of light tone with dark edges where the paint has been pushed to the edge of the shape created by the flow of the liquid. They are useful for creating patterned silks for appliqué, bonding and so forth.

24 *Poplars at Ness Gardens, Wirral*
Antifusant was used with silk paints to create
the lightest colours of the water. Details were
added with machine embroidery.

8 Using Painted Silk for Clothes and Accessories

Silk's strength and lustre and the fact that it hangs so beautifully make it ideal for certain types of garment and accessories. It can also be used to appliqué on to garments to add points of interest or areas that coordinate with bags or scarves.

You do not need large-scale equipment to enjoy making a silk garment or to add a dash of colour to a sweatshirt, blouse or T-shirt. Embroidery hoops or small frames are sufficient to decorate the silk, which can be used to highlight a plain garment of any compatible fabric.

The first consideration is the weight of the silk. I once made a lovely scarf and carefully handrolled the edges, but I became so involved with the design and colour that I forgot to think about the weight of the fabric. It was a heavyweight habutai, which did not sit well as a scarf. However, I made it into a tie instead, so all was not lost. Silk is so versatile that it need never be wasted. Even left-over snippets can be used in embroidery or on other items. When you are sewing silk, you must remember to press garment seams flat on both sides, then press open the inside seam edges, and always use a fine needle and silk thread on silk garments.

Colour photograph 25 shows some garments for which painted silk of the same design was used. The tie, coordinated shirt, appliquéd sweatshirt and scarf were all made from fabric that was painted with a design based on scraps of fabric loosely stitched together in a haphazard, patchwork effect; a detail is shown in colour photograph 26. I painted a small sample on a hoop to see how the idea would work. Then I followed the processes already described and painted the pattern on a larger scale. I needed to paint two large frames to have enough silk.

CHOOSING A FRAME
When you work on a large frame it is important that it is not too shallow. I

use a frame that is 3in (7.5cm) deep, so when there is a weight of paint on the silk, it does not sink and touch the work surface below. If your frame is not deep enough, the weight of paint on the silk can cause the fabric to sink and stick to your work surface, which can be disastrous. If you do not have a sufficiently deep frame, raise your frame by standing it on jar lids or something similar, which have been stuck down with double-sided tape so that they do not slip.

The size of the garment you plan to make will, of course, dictate the size of the frame needed. I have found that a frame 28 × 28in (71 × 71cm) and 3in (7.5cm) deep is large enough for a tie, a small appliqué motif, or a waistcoat front. A frame of these dimensions will also accommodate a reasonably sized scarf.

CHOOSING THE SILK

For the garments illustrated in colour photograph 25 I used two different weights of silk – a heavyweight for the tie, appliqué motif and shirt pocket and a medium weight for the scarf.

When you make a scarf you must also consider whether to use a ready-rolled silk or to roll the edges yourself. I find that ready-rolled silk is difficult to paint because it is tricky to get right to the edge of the scarf through the pins and to paint the silk evenly right up to the edge. Ready-rolled scarves are, however, ideal for designs that involve the use of an embroidery frame when the background is left plain.

PAINTING THE SILK

Stretch the silk over the frame, remembering that it should be raised at least 2in (5cm) above your work surface.

Pour the paints into a clean palette or jar and, if possible, use a different brush for each colour. I used 1in (2.5cm) brushes for the design shown in colour photograph 26. When you execute a design of this nature you have to work quite quickly so that the paints merge into each other and there are no nasty tidemarks. It is easy to spoil the colours by not cleaning your brush thoroughly, and using separate brushes helps to avoid this.

Using the lightest colour first – in this case it was yellow – apply dabs of paint to different areas of the silk to create an even distribution of yellow shapes. Repeat the process with red and try to manipulate the colours so that they blend into each other without obliterating all the white background. White adds important highlights to any design, and it intensifies the effect of the other colours by contrast. Follow the same procedure with blue. You are, in effect, simply blocking in the primary colours in a very simple way. They will bleed into each other to create secondaries.

Leave the silk to dry flat overnight. Take it off the frame, iron it to fix the paints and replace it on the frame.

Now prepare some Deka fabric paints. I used blue, white and red for this

25   A tie, coordinated shirt, appliquéd
sweatshirt and scarf made with painted silk.
The fabric paint was applied with a gutta nib.

26   A detail of the fabric used for the clothes
illustrated in colour photograph 25.

111

colour scheme. The paint must be poured into a bottle and applied with a narrow gutta nib. The plastic bottles used for gutta as described in Chapter 1 are ideal. It is a good idea to keep a set of plastic bottles of fabric paint to hand so that when you need a colour, you can simply attach a lid with a gutta nib already in position and apply the paint as required. In this design the fabric paint was simply drawn on using a random zigzag pattern.

Leave the silk on the frame until the fabric paint is absolutely dry. Overnight is best. When you are sure that the paints are quite dry, fix them by ironing the fabric on the wrong side with the iron on medium heat. If you want to add a personal touch, add your name or initials to the fabric before you remove the silk from the frame.

MAKING A SCARF

This is a simple matter of handrolling a fine hem along the edge of the scarf. Figs. 81 and 82 illustrate the process, which will be made easier if you machine stitch very close to the edge of the silk before you begin.

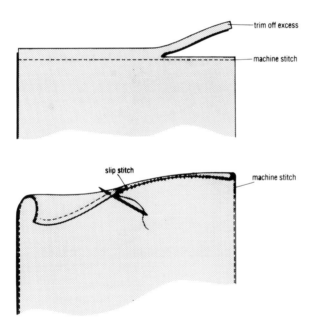

Fig. 81 Before you handroll a scarf, machine stitch around the edge and neatly trim off the excess.

Fig. 82 Dampen your fingers and roll down the edge of the silk. Use slip stitch to hold it in place.

MAKING A TIE

Commercial patterns can be used and are relatively straightforward to follow. I unpicked an old tie and used it to make a card template. The pattern pieces must be laid diagonally across the fabric as they have to be cut on the cross (Fig. 83). Use lightweight Vilene for interfacing and tack it to the silk; iron-on Vilene does not seem to work so well with silk. I sewed up the tie following the lines of stitching on the old tie and was surprised and pleased at the result. Colourful ties and bows are popular with all ages and add a dash to a plain outfit. A hand-painted silk tie makes a very attractive and distinctive gift.

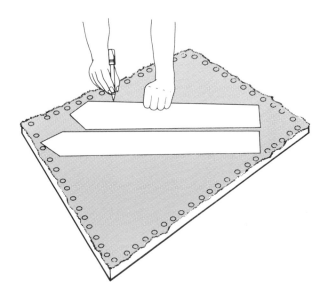

Fig. 83 Lay the pattern diagonally across the silk, stretched on the frame, and outline with fabric pen. Remove silk and cut out.

ADDING SILK TO A POCKET

If you want to coordinate a shirt or blouse with a tie look through the pieces that are left after cutting out the tie. When you find a suitable piece, cut a strip from it that is slightly longer than and double the width of the hem on the shirt pocket. Unpick the hem of the pocket (Fig. 84) and pin the band of silk to it. With right sides together, tack and machine stitch it in position (Fig. 85), and then fold the band of silk over along the fold lines of the original hem, turning it under at the sides. Pin, tack and top stitch it so that the pocket is in its original position (Fig. 86).

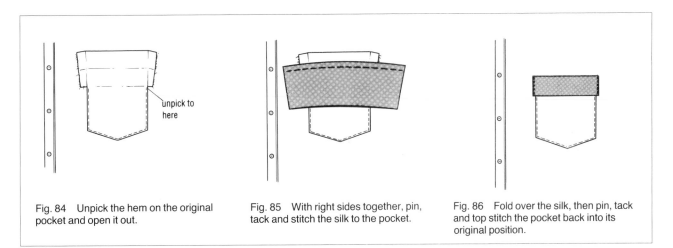

Fig. 84 Unpick the hem on the original pocket and open it out.

Fig. 85 With right sides together, pin, tack and stitch the silk to the pocket.

Fig. 86 Fold over the silk, then pin, tack and top stitch the pocket back into its original position.

APPLIQUÉ USING PAINTED SILK

The appliqué design on the sweatshirt (Fig. 87) matches the scarf and was extremely simple to apply.

It is a good idea to cut out a template and stick it to the garment with double-sided tape so that you can adjust the position, shape and size of the motif. When you are happy with it, mark the position with a 'disappearing' fabric pen and proceed with your appliqué.

Proprietary adhesive backing materials such as Bondaweb have made appliquéing very easy. You can bond some white pre-shrunk, backing fabric on to the silk, apply Bondaweb to the background fabric, cut out the shape while the backing paper is in place, peel it off and iron the appliqué into position.

If you prefer, you can tack the silk to a white backing fabric then tack the whole thing to the garment. When the appliqué is firmly in position, stitch it into place using straight stitch. Then trim all edges and satin stitch.

The design I used on the sweatshirt was so simple that I managed with the machine set for straightforward satin stitch. There was no need to stretch it in a hoop as for machine embroidery, although you can, if you wish, use a hoop for extra stability.

Fig. 87 It is very easy to apply an appliqué motif to the front of a sweatshirt.

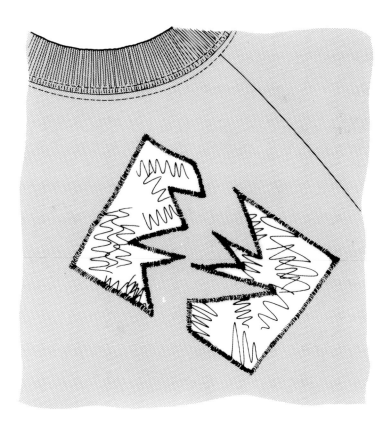

27 The anemones were worked in silk paint on silk that had been soaked in salt solution and allowed to dry naturally before the details were added in fabric paint. The motif was appliquéd to a sweatshirt.

APPLIQUÉ USING MACHINE EMBROIDERY

Colour photograph 27 shows a sweatshirt with a painting of anemones appliquéd to it. As we saw in Chapter 7, the use of salt solutions offers some interesting opportunities to work as they obviate the need for gutta lines altogether. The silk was soaked overnight in a strong salt solution. It was dried thoroughly in fresh air and stretched on a frame. I painted the anemones free-hand, using reference sketches I had made, but you could trace or draw any design in fabric pen on the silk. I used Deka silk paints for the flowers, leaving some silk unpainted for highlights. Then I left it to dry for 12 hours. I fixed the paints by ironing and washed the silk thoroughly to remove all traces of salt. I then re-stretched the silk using silk pins so that I could add some leaf and flower details using Deka fabric paint with a very narrow gutta nib. I mixed several greens for the leaves and used black for the flower centres. I then left the silk to dry for another 12 hours, after which I ironed it to fix the paints. The design was then ready to appliqué.

I did not want simply to machine an oblong piece of silk to the sweatshirt because I wanted the painting to merge into the fabric. This meant that I had to machine embroider around the design using satin stitch, and so I used a strengthening fabric as well as a backing cotton so that it would be easier to stitch. Proprietary strengthening fabrics are widely available under a variety of names – Sew and Tear, for example – and they help to stabilize thin fabrics when appliquéing. I used some pre-shrunk cotton as a backing for the anemone picture, and I tacked it in place along the diagonals. I had painted the anemones on an oblong frame, so I cut the cotton to the same size as the frame. White cotton backing helps to throw up the colour on painted silk of all weights, so it is a good idea to use it even if you are working on a white background, and it is essential if you are appliquéing on a coloured background.

The next stage was to pin the painted silk with its cotton backing to the sweatshirt. I put the sweatshirt on and stood in front of a mirror to judge the right position, but if it is a large piece of appliqué, you might need a friend to help you. You must be careful to avoid pins when you take off the garment. Double-sided tape is a useful alternative for small motifs, but pins do a better job on larger pieces, even if they are hazardous. The final stage before tacking was to place a piece of stabilizing fabric, the same size as the silk, inside the sweatshirt, aligning it with the silk. Then the four layers – silk, cotton, sweatshirt and stabilizer – were tacked diagonally. Always work from the centre out so that the whole thing sits smoothly.

Stitching the design using the machine embroidery facility meant that it had to be in an embroidery hoop. I used an 8in (20cm) hoop, with the inner ring bound with cotton tape to stop the fabric slipping. The fabric layers had to be adjusted gently but firmly until they were all as taut as possible. I then stitched around the whole design with straight stitch, moving the frame three times to complete the design. Every time the frame was moved, I had to take care that the fabric was as taut as possible and that the screw of the outer hoop was tightened with a screw driver.

After I had finished the straight stitching, I used small, sharp embroidery scissors to trim away all the excess fabric to within an ⅛in (3mm) of the stitching line.

The next stage of the process was the satin stitching. I used width 3 for this design. I again set up the fabric in the hoop, and satin stitched along the straight stitch, using the stitch line as a guide. Satin stitch using the machine embroidery facility is ideal for complicated appliqué shapes as it enables you to manoeuvre smoothly around any type of shape.

Finally, the tacking was removed, the loose ends finished off and the excess stabilizer fabric torn away.

ADDING APPLIQUÉ TO A T-SHIRT

The design for the T-shirt illustrated in colour photograph 28 and in Fig. 88 was carried out in two stages, using transparent gutta to block out areas of silk. It is an easy painting process and one that can be adjusted to any type of design.

Stretch some medium or heavyweight silk over a frame that is sufficiently large to accommodate the size of your appliqué. Use a 1in (2.5cm) wide brush to paint transparent gutta over the silk so that rectangular shapes are blocked out at random intervals. Allow the gutta to dry naturally. This is extremely important – if you try to speed up the process the gutta will not wash out easily.

When the gutta is dry, which may take 24 hours, apply Deka paint at random with a 1in (2½cm) brush. Overlay paint on top of the gutta areas to create a mishmash of colourful shapes. When I was preparing this design, I was thinking about Greek columns, particularly Ionic ones, with their scrolls at the top. The patterns in all Greek and Roman capitals are very beautiful and a rich design source.

When the paint is completely dry, fix it in the usual way and carefully wash out the transparent gutta. Roll the silk in a towel, iron it dry, and re-stretch it on the frame. Then draw in additional gutta lines. In this case I drew ribbon-like shapes, some overlapping, inside the white areas left by the original gutta and carefully outlined the edges of the shapes to stop any paint spreading on to the areas already painted.

Paint in the newly drawn shapes and, again, leave to dry thoroughly. Fix the paints and wash out all the gutta, iron and re-stretch the fabric. Now take some Deka permanent fabric paint. In the motif used on the T-shirt I used black, and, with a narrow nib, I applied further designs to the silk. Here I applied spiral shapes that were reminiscent of Ionic capitals. Allow the paint to dry, fix it by ironing and you have a completely washable piece of silk.

To appliqué the motif on to a T-shirt, follow the method described for appliquéing painted silk described above. For this simple, angular design the machine can be used on the ordinary stitch mechanism, and you can use a hoop for stability if you wish, as T-shirt fabric is light and stretchy. Sew your appliqué in place with straight (or running) stitch first.

Fig. 88   The design appliquéd to the T-shirt that is illustrated in colour photograph 28.

28   Detail of the design appliquéd to a T-shirt. The pattern was worked on silk with transparent gutta and fabric paint.

A PAINTED WAISTCOAT

The colourful waistcoast that is illustrated in colour photograph 29 was made from a commercial pattern. I used the same frame as for the scarf – that is, one measuring 28 × 28in (71 × 71cm). The painting process was very similar to the one used for the scarf. I painted overlapping oval shapes on to the silk using a limited palette of primary colours together with green Deka paint. When the silk paints were dry, I used a narrow gutta nib to draw into the design with fabric paint. I fixed the paint by ironing and laid the waistcoat front pattern pieces on to the silk according to the instructions. After cutting out, I made up the waistcoat, following the pattern requirements. I used polyester satin for the lining and for the back, but used painted silk for the strap, which made an attractive contrast.

I used an overall, abstract pattern in this design, but you could outline any shape – a tie or a waistcoat, for instance – with gutta, remembering to leave a seam allowance, and then gutta a precise representational design within that outline.

If you have the time and the patience you could hand stitch accessories such as bags or purses. These tend to be luxury items, and they demand very careful planning and a lot of painstaking work.

119

HAND STITCHING A SILK BAG

Colour photograph 30 shows an exquisite hand-worked bag by Lynda Jowers. It was inspired by an Indian bag that Lynda had seen being made out of an Indian textile when she visited Bhuj in Gujarat.

The form of the bag is relatively simple – it is based on a square, and the four corners are brought together so that the fabric falls in soft folds. Both the quilted design on the exterior of the bag and the design on the lining are based on drawings and paintings taken from studies of Indian buildings. Several aspects of Indian architecture from the Havelis buildings feature in the composite pattern; these can be seen in Fig. 89. The colour scheme was chosen to reflect the cream and neutral sand tones of these buildings, with their highlights of turquoise and peachy-rust.

When the design (Fig. 90) had been worked out, a photocopy was made of the whole thing, and this photocopy was then enlarged to the actual size of the design to be worked, which was approximately 25 × 25in (63 × 63cm). There are different ways of doing this. Some printers and stationery shops

Fig. 89   Some of the preliminary drawings for the hand-quilted crêpe de Chine bag that is shown in colour photograph 30.

120

Fig. 90   The composite photocopy that was used for tracing the design on to the crêpe de Chine with a fabric pen.

have photocopiers that can enlarge designs to a very large size. If you have access to a less sophisticated copier you can cut up your photocopy, enlarge each piece to exactly the same size and reassemble your design. Alternatively, you can enlarge your design using the grid method described in Chapter 3, but this is more time consuming and laborious.

The main structure of the design was traced on to the cream crêpe de Chine with a fabric pen, and the silk was then tacked on to lightweight polyester wadding with a muslin backing.

The hand quilting was done with a range of turquoise and peach-coloured silk threads. Most of the lines were worked in running stitch, but the edges and some other motifs were worked in chain stitch to give additional strength and to accentuate some parts of the design.

Three types of quilting were used on the bag. The whole area was wadded – that is, it was quilted – with running stitches through three layers including the polyester wadding, but some areas have been given additional interest by using trapunto and Italian quilting. Trapunto is a type of quilting in which parts of a design are given extra padding, which is inserted by cutting the

29 A waistcoat, made from a commercial pattern, in painted silk with detail added in fabric paints.

30 A painted and hand-quilted crêpe de Chine bag, which was made using gutta and salt-texturing techniques.

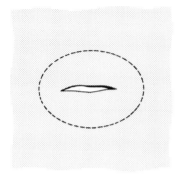

Fig. 91   The first stage in trapunto quilting is to cut a slit in the backing layer, which may be muslin or cotton, of the shape or area of the design to be padded.

Fig. 92   Carefully insert the extra wadding – the point of a knitting needle is useful – making sure that it is evenly distributed and that no unevenness appears on the right side.

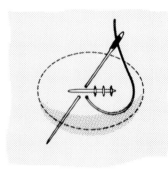

Fig. 93   Oversew the edges of the slit with small stitches.

back layer (the muslin) and inserting extra wadding, to vary the visual effect (Figs. 91, 92 and 93). Italian quilting involves running cord through parallel lines of stitching so that it shows between the first layer of silk and the wadding and gives a raised effect to any linear areas of stitching (Fig. 94).

The lining silk used for the bag was lightweight ecru habutai. The design for this was traced directly off the original photocopy, which was covered with sticky-backed transparent plastic. The silk was stuck to the work surface with masking tape and the design outlined in clear gutta, a method that works well with transparent gutta. The habutai was stretched on a frame and painted in Deka paints – azure, sienna, yellow, ochre and bordeaux – and the ecru of the silk gave the colours a muted appearance. Some parts of the design were treated with salt while the paint was wet to create areas of texture and contrast in the pattern.

When the quilting and lining were complete, the finishing touches were added. Kumihimo braid was used to edge the bag and as a shoulder strap. Kumihimo is traditional Japanese braid that is made on a piece of equipment called a marudai. The same colour silks were used for the braids as for the quilting, with fine threads being used for the braiding along the edges of the top of the bag and thicker ones for the shoulder strap.

Whatever type of project you are embarking upon, it is wise to begin with a simple, small-scale example. I always keep silk on a small hoop to practise any new techniques of painting or embroidery. If you follow the correct procedures – stretch the silk properly, fix the paints and follow the pattern instructions – practically any garment or accessory can be made using any type of design or effect. One of the beauties of this combination of media is that there is always a new challenge.

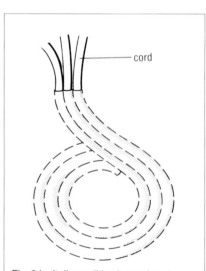

cord

Fig. 94   Italian quilting is used to give a raised effect in linear patterns. Wash the quilting cord before you use it, as it will shrink. The cord is inserted from the back between parallel lines of running stitches.

Further Reading

SILK PAINTING
Dawson, Pam (ed.), *The Art of Painting on Silk*, Search Press, Tunbridge Wells, 1987
Kennedy, Jill and Varrall, Jane, *Painting on Silk*, Dryad Press, Leicester, 1988

HAND EMBROIDERY
Beaney, Jan, *Stitches: New Approaches*, B.T. Batsford, London, 1987
Beaney, Jan, *The Art of the Needle*, Century, London, 1988
Messent, Jan, *Embroidery and Nature*, B.T. Batsford, London, 1983
Morell, Anne, *Using Simple Embroidery Stitches*, B.T. Batsford, London, 1985

MACHINE EMBROIDERY
Campbell Harding, Valerie and Watts, Pamela, *Machine Embroidery Stitch Techniques*, B.T. Batsford, London, 1990
Clucas, Joy, *The New Machine Embroidery*, David & Charles, Newton Abbot, 1987
Holt, Alison, *Machine Embroidered Landscapes*, B.T. Batsford, London, 1990
Hubbard, Liz, *Thread Painting*, David & Charles, Newton Abbot, 1988
Warren, Verina, *Landscape in Embroidery*, B.T. Batsford, London, 1986

GENERAL
Beck, Thomasina, *The Embroiderer's Garden*, David & Charles, Newton Abbot, 1988
Box, Richard, *Drawing and Design for Embroidery*, B.T. Batsford, London, 1988
Campbell Harding, Valerie, *Flowers and Plants in Embroidery*, B.T. Batsford, London, 1986
Thompson, Frances and Tony, *Synthetic Dyeing*, David & Charles, Newton Abbot, 1987

THE SILK INDUSTRY
Bush, Sarah, *The Silk Industry*, Shire Publications, Princes Risborough, 1987
Sanderson, Kylie (ed.), *British Fabrics*, Columbus Press, London, 1987

Index